simple elegance

Furnishing with Fabric

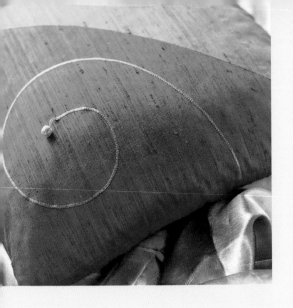

simple

Compiled by Dawn Anderson

elegance

Furnishing with Fabric

Martingale
& COMPANY

WOODINVILLE, WASHINGTON

Credits

President . . . . Nancy J. Martin

CEO . . . . Daniel J. Martin

Publisher . . . . Jane Hamada

Editorial Director . . . . Mary V. Green

Editorial Project Manager . . . Tina Cook

Technical Editor . . . . . . Dawn Anderson

Copy Editor . . . . Candie Frankel

Design and
Production Manager. . . . . . . Stan Green

Illustrators . . . . . Mary Newell DePalma,
    Roberta Frauwirth, Jil Johänson,
    Judy Love

Photographer . . . . Carl Tremblay

Cover Designer . . . . Stan Green

Text Designer . . . . Trina Stahl

Simple Elegance: Furnishing with Fabric

© 2001 by Martingale & Company

The contributor credits that appear on page 96 are hereby made a part of this copyright page.

Martingale & Company
20205 144th Avenue NE
Woodinville, WA 98072-8478 USA
www.martingale-pub.com

Printed in the United States of America
06 05 04 03 02 01   6 5 4 3 2 1

Mission Statement

We are dedicated to providing quality products and service by working together to inspire creativity and to enrich the lives we touch.

Library of Congress Cataloging-in-Publication Data

Simple elegance: furnishing with fabric / compiled by Dawn Anderson.
    p.   cm.
    ISBN 1-56477-373-6
    1. Household linens.   2. Textile fabrics in interior decoration.   I. Anderson, Dawn.
TT387.S546 2001
646.2'1—dc21
                                                    00–048061

Contents

introduction

FABRIC FURNISHINGS help bring a feeling of comfort to a home by providing an element of softness. Use pillows to create a cozy corner on a sofa, or hang a valance to soften the hard lines of a window frame. Decorating with fabrics also provides lots of opportunities for coordinating your decorating scheme. You can easily use leftover fabric scraps from a bedding ensemble to create a matching lampshade or pillow.

This book is a compilation of several fabric projects. A few require sewing experience, some involve only minimal sewing, and others are put together by simply gluing or stapling. A few of the projects incorporate non-fabric techniques such as painting or wire bending. Explore the possibilities offered here, and create some unique fabric furnishings for your home. Start with one of the many pillows offered in this book. Choose a pyramid-shaped pillow for a contemporary feel, or for a very ornate look make the Victorian round pillow from silk and tapestry and add lots of trimmings. Instructions for table coverings and bed coverings are also included in this book. The holiday table wrap is an easy table accent that can be made in a couple of hours and adds a festive touch to holiday gatherings. Learn to dress up bed linens with a few rows of stitched trims along the borders, or make a scalloped duvet cover and shams. For windows, create the look of casual elegance following the instructions for making silk drapery panels. Or, for a low-sew window treatment, try the faux-embroidered curtain, made with photo-transferred leaf designs. Learn how to make a loose-fitting slipcover for an armchair or how to make a decorative footstool. Whatever your decorating needs, you are sure to find lots of inspiring fabric ideas in this book. Customize the projects shown here, choosing fabric colors that work in your decorating scheme. You will find plenty of projects that will help bring a cozy warmth to your home.

CHINESE SILK PILLOWS

Two brass dragon charms face off in mirror image on each pillow front.

chinese silk pillows

By Dawn Anderson

HERE'S A MULTIFABRIC pillow cover that is deceptively easy to make. The meticulous "piecework" is an illusion that is achieved by layering.

The base fabric is a cranberry silk dupioni, which I overlaid with gold-dotted organza. A rectangle cut out of the middle of the organza lets the silk show through, creating the two-fabric look. To conceal the raw edges, I simply arranged strips of ribbon around the cutout like a frame. Be sure to choose a wide ribbon to allow some play when you work out the frame dimensions. You'll also need to decide which part of the ribbon design looks best in the mitered corners. Once the ribbon frame is created, you simply topstitch it into place.

materials

Makes two pillows

- 45"-wide fabric:
    - ¾ yard cranberry silk dupioni
    - ¾ yard cranberry organza with gold dots
- 2¼ yard 1½" cranberry/gold ribbon (MOKUBA #4604)
- 3⅜ yard narrow gold rope welting
- Eight 4" gold tassels
- Four 2" brass dragon charms (for two mirror images)
- Thread to match fabrics
- Two 12" x 16" pillow forms
- E-6000 glue

You'll also need: sewing machine, iron and ironing board, rotary cutter, clear acrylic grid ruler, self-healing cutting mat, chalk pencil, sewing shears, hand-sewing needle, pins, darning needle, jewelry pliers, pencil, toothpicks, and scrap cardboard.

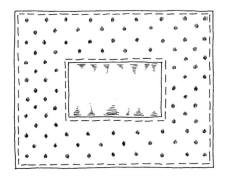

A. Baste organza frame over silk dupioni rectangle.

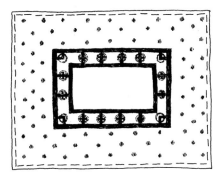

B. Topstitch ribbon frame over raw edges of organza.

instructions

1. Cut fabrics. For each pillow, cut two 13" x 17" rectangles from silk dupioni and two from organza. Draft and cut a 4½" x 8" cardboard template. Center template on one organza piece and cut same-size opening.

2. Baste fabrics. Lay each silk rectangle flat, right side up. Lay organza rectangle right side up on top. Hand-baste around outer edges and around window opening (illustration A).

3. Create ribbon frame. Pin ribbon around window opening, concealing cut edge of organza. Adjust so ribbon designs are symmetrical and will meet neatly at corners; mark with pins. For each miter join, stack two ribbons, right sides together, and stitch at 45° angle. Trim excess and press seam open. Pin completed ribbon frame over window opening, and hand-baste all around. Topstitch along both edges (illustration B).

4. Glue on dragon charms. Using jewelry pliers, bend two dragon charms so they lie flat. Center charms within window, facing each other, and mark with chalk pencil. Apply glue to back of each charm with toothpick and press in place. Let dry.

> ► Designer's Tip
>
> If you are unable to find cranberry organza with gold dots for the outer frame of the pillow, you can substitute any gold or cranberry fabric of your choice. To achieve a transparent, layered look similar to the one shown here, use a plain cranberry organza and add gold dots using a thick, metallic gold acrylic paint.

5. Stitch pillow. Pin rope welting to edge of pillow front. Stitch all around using zipper foot, clipping tape at corners so cord lies smooth (illustration C). Pin pillow front and back right sides together. Stitch all around just inside previous stitching, leaving 9" opening; do not turn right side out.

6. Finish pillow. Thread tassel hanging cord through darning needle. Place tassel inside pillow cover, draw needle out at tip of one corner, and pull snug. Machine-stitch across tassel hanger to secure (illustration D). Repeat at each corner. Turn cover right side out, insert pillow form, and slipstitch opening closed.

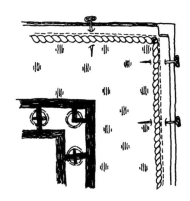

C. Stitch rope welting to outer edges of pillow front.

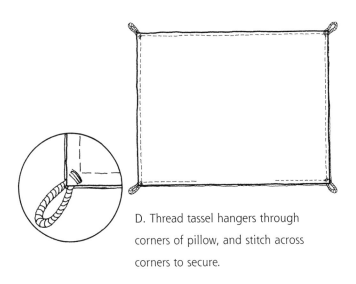

D. Thread tassel hangers through corners of pillow, and stitch across corners to secure.

► Designer's Tip

For an invisible cord join, try this: Stitch down the tape all around, leaving a 1½" tail at each end. Pick out the manufacturer's stitches on each tail to release the cord from the tape. Unravel the cord from both tails, and overlap cords from one end over cords on the other end. Restitch over this area.

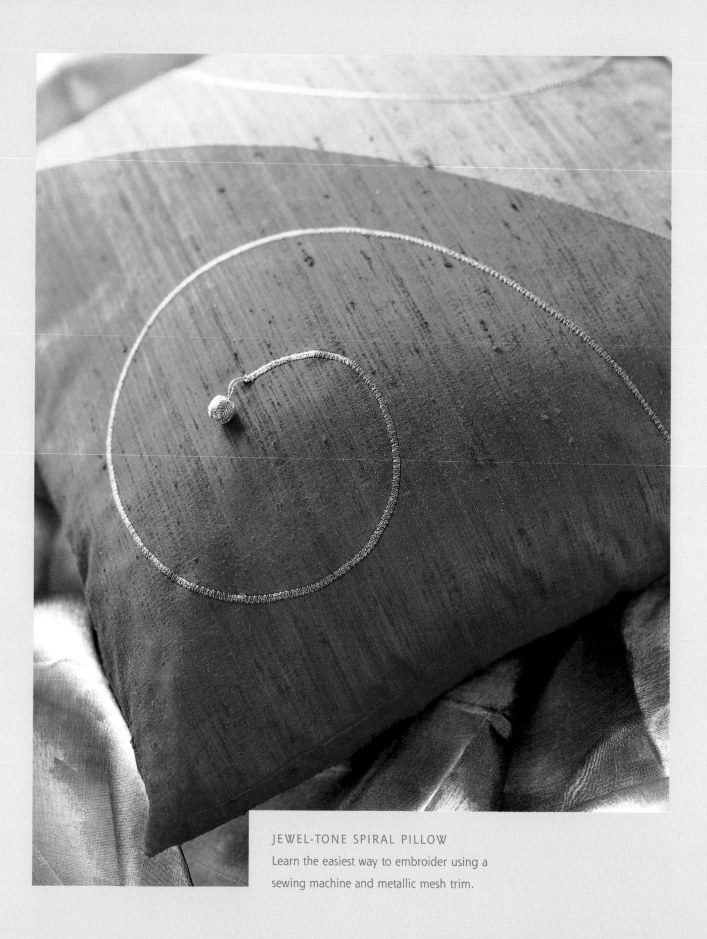

JEWEL-TONE SPIRAL PILLOW
Learn the easiest way to embroider using a
sewing machine and metallic mesh trim.

jewel-tone spiral pillow

By Dawn Anderson

THIS PILLOW DESIGN juxtaposes a vivid diagonal division of color with soft, swirling curves of metallic trim. The spiral appliqué is created by machine stitching a fine zigzag over a piece of metallic mesh trim that is positioned in a swirl.

To achieve inconspicuous stitching, practice sewing the trim onto scrap fabric. Adjust your machine settings to determine the proper width of the zigzag stitch needed to clear the trim on each side; you don't want the needle to actually pierce the trim. If the mesh trim spreads or flattens while you are stitching, pull gently on the trim to ease the threads back together.

Though I used cranberry and green dupioni silk, you could adapt the colors to your home; just choose two colors with a similar tone or saturation.

materials

Makes one 16"-square pillow

- 45"-wide silk dupioni:
    - ½ yard cranberry
    - ½ yard green
- 1⅜ yards ⅛"-wide silver mesh trim
- Two ⅜" silver mesh balls or beads
- Thread to match fabrics and trim
- Nylon monofilament thread
- 16"-square pillow form
- Clear nail polish

You'll also need: spiral pattern (see page 15), access to photocopier with enlarger, sewing machine, iron and ironing board, rotary cutter, clear acrylic grid ruler, self-healing cutting mat, tear-away stabilizer, hand-sewing needle, pins, scissors, transfer paper, and pencil.

instructions

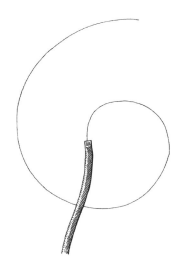

A. Tack down the trim end at the start of the spiral.

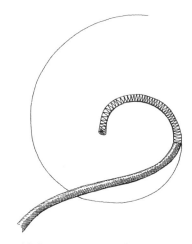

B. Fold the trim onto itself and secure with a zigzag stitch.

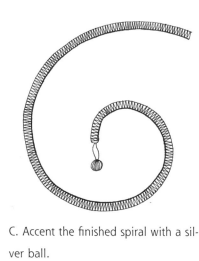

C. Accent the finished spiral with a silver ball.

1. **Prepare pillow front.** Photocopy pattern (page 15), enlarging by 200%. From either silk, cut one 16¾" square for pillow back. From both, cut one 17½" square, then cut square in half diagonally. Pin two contrasting triangles right sides together and edges matching. (The two remaining triangles are not used, but could be saved for a second pillow.) Stitch diagonal edge, making ½" seam. Press seam open. Lay piece flat, right side up. Position spiral pattern on one triangle, aligning corners and seamline. Slip transfer paper between layers, and trace design with pencil to mark fabric. Repeat process to mark remaining triangle. Back each design with tear-away stabilizer, inserting pins from the right side.

2. **Sew mesh spirals.** Cut silver mesh trim in half. Seal one end of each length with clear nail polish for ½". Let dry 5 minutes, then trim off ⅜". Hold sealed end against spiral's innermost point, so trim faces away from spiral. Using monofilament thread, machine-tack trim to fabric ⅛" from trim end (illustration A). Stop with needle in down position in fabric only. Fold trim back on itself to conceal stitching. Using short zigzag (26 stitches per inch), stitch down trim following marked spiral design (illustration B). Cut off excess trim even with fabric edge. Repeat process to stitch second spiral. Gently tear away stabilizer from wrong side. You do not need to remove paper caught under the stitches.

3. **Assemble pillow.** Place pillow front and back right sides together on cutting mat. Align pattern on one corner, and cut along taper lines with rotary cutter. Repeat at each corner (tapering this way prevents the pillow corners from flaring). Machine-stitch ½" from edges all around, leaving 12" opening on one side for turning. Clip corners diagonally. Turn right side out. Tack silver ball or bead to each inner spiral (illustration C). Insert pillow form, and slipstitch opening closed.

> ► **Designer's Tip**
>
> To get the most fabric mileage, make two pillows. Back one pillow with green silk and the other with cranberry. For a luxurious feel, use down-and-feather pillow forms.

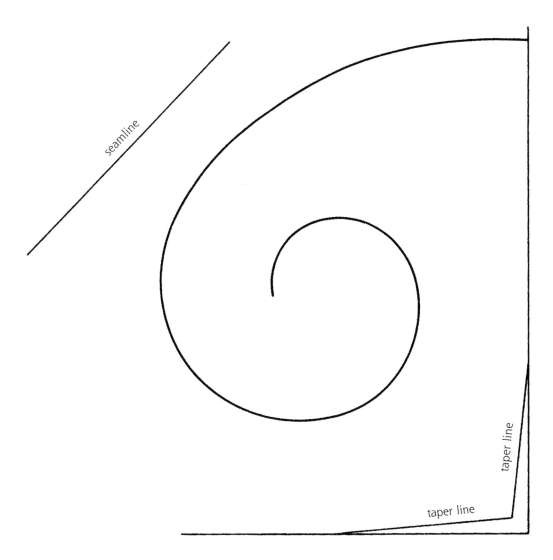

seamline

taper line

taper line

Jewel-Tone Spiral Pillow Pattern
Photocopy at 200%.

Assemble an unlimited assortment of ball-shaped pillows using one simple pattern.

tasseled ball pillows

By Candie Frankel

The construction of this pillow is very simple: It is sewn from eight lozenge-shaped panels that are cut using one pattern. The design's versatility comes in mixing and matching the fabrics.

For each pillow shown, I bought three fabrics in total. For four of the eight panels I used a tan polka-dot sateen. For the four remaining panels, I selected two contrasting decorator-weight fabrics. I purposely varied the color, pattern, and texture of each pillow's fabrics. On one pillow, for example, soft graphic images are positioned side by side with the polka-dot sateen. By pairing off like panels, I was able to create large blocks of color in a beach-ball style.

For a busier effect with these same fabrics, I could have alternated the eight panels so that no two like fabrics ended up side by side. For less variation, I could have used similar textures, a single fabric design in several different colors, or assorted patterns that share the same color tone. You could also mix three highly contrasting solid-colored fabrics or choose eight coordinating fabrics and cut one panel from each. Moving in a different direction, imagine the pillow sewn from a solid-colored fabric, such as a plush velvet, with contrasting tassels. With this one-panel technique, the design configurations are virtually endless. To ensure that my pillows worked together as a set, I made the tan polka-dot fabric a constant in all three.

No matter what fabric configuration you choose, most ball-pillow designs require that the panels be cut on the bias. This cutting direction allows more all-around give, or stretch, along the seams, which enhances the rounded, globelike form. You may find, however, that certain fabrics need to be cut on the straight grain in order to present the pattern a certain way. The harlequin diamonds used on one of my pillows, for instance, presented this problem. The diamonds are more dramatic viewed straight on, meaning the panels could not be cut on the bias. You can still make your pillow using this type of fabric, but be aware that the straight-grain pieces will not have the same give as those cut on the bias, and the pillow will not have the same overall roundness. On the harlequin pillow, the diamond fabric "bumps out" slightly near the ends, whereas the bias-cut pieces lie flatter and smoother. To mask this slight tendency, I ran button-and-carpet thread through the pillow and back, cinching the entire ball and lightly dimpling the ends.

materials

Makes three pillows

- ¾ yard 60"-wide fabric
- 6 coordinating fabrics, 14" x 18" each
- Six 4" tassels
- 18 ounces fiberfill
- Thread to match fabrics
- Button-and-carpet thread

You'll also need: ball pillow pattern (see page 20), access to photocopier with enlarger, sewing machine, rotary cutter, self-healing cutting mat, scissors, ruler, sewing needle, 5" doll-making needle, seam ripper, and pins.

instructions

1. Prepare ball-pillow pattern. Photocopy pattern (see page 20), enlarging it to measure 14" from tip to tip. (When enlarged, the pattern should fit diagonally on an 8½" x 14" piece of paper.) Cut out pattern with scissors.

2. Cut and sort fabric pieces. Lay main fabric yardage face up on cutting mat. Following layout diagram (left), pin pattern to fabric on bias and cut out with rotary cutter. Repeat to cut twelve pieces total. Then repeat to cut two pieces from each of six coordinating fabrics. Divide main fabric pieces into three groups of four. To complete palette for each pillow, select and add two pairs of coordinating fabrics (four pieces) to each group for a total of eight pieces.

3. Sew pairs together. For each pillow, staystitch any two matching pieces ½" from one curved edge between dots (illustration A). Stack pieces

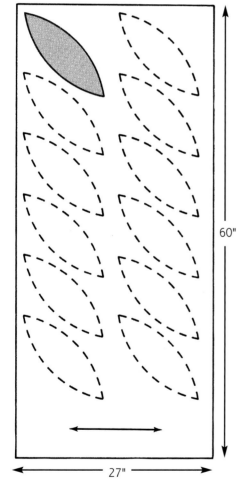

60"

27"

Layout Diagram

right sides together so staystitching matches, then stitch from dots out to ends. Reinforce these short seams by stitching again ⅜" from edge (illustration B). Stack remaining pieces in pairs and stitch ½" from one edge, then stitch again ⅜" from edge (illustration C).

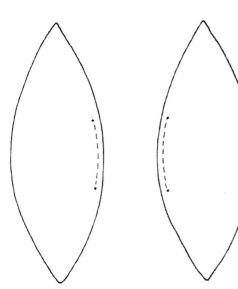

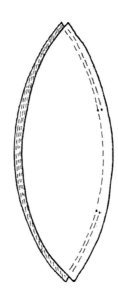

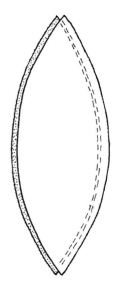

A. Staystitch two matching pieces between the dots.

B. Sew the pieces together, but leave the staystitched section open. Reinforce the seams.

C. Join the three remaining pairs by stitching along one edge. Then add a second row of stitching for reinforcement.

➤ Staystitch Defined

A row of directional machine stitching, usually placed just inside the seam line, to prevent curved or sloped fabric edges from stretching out of shape. In the ball pillow, the staystitching also helps you keep a neat edge when slip stitching the pillow closed.

4. Assemble pillow. For each pillow, sew four pairs together so fabrics alternate beach-ball style. Stitch and reinforce seams, as in step 3 (illustration D).

5. Insert fiberfill. Turn pillow cover right side out. Insert fiberfill through opening until ball is well rounded. Slipstitch opening closed (illustration E).

6. Cinch pillow and attach tassels. Using doll-making needle, draw button-and-carpet thread through center of pillow and back (illustration F). Pull thread ends lightly to cinch pillow, then tie off. Use seam ripper to poke tassel cord into each dimpled end, then hand-tack to secure (illustration G).

➤ Designer's Tip

This is a good project for using up leftover fabric from larger decorating projects. Fabric left over from sewing draperies may not be sufficient to make a full pillow, for instance, but you might be able to work your scraps into a ball pillow.

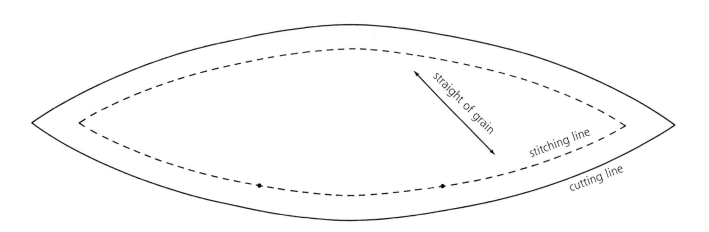

straight of grain

stitching line

cutting line

Tasseled Ball Pillow Pattern. Photocopy at 200% (to measure 14" long).

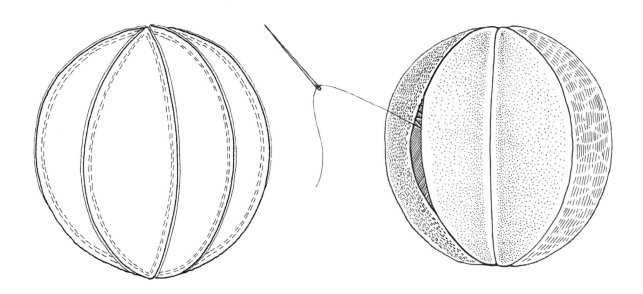

D. Sew all four pairs together beach-ball style.

E. Turn the pillow right side out, stuff it with fiberfill, and sew the pillow closed.

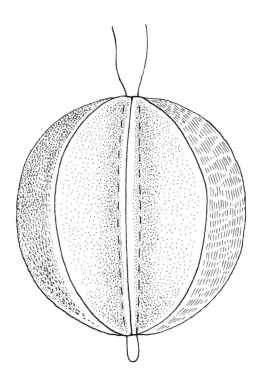

F. Draw carpet thread through the ball and back, pull it lightly to cinch, and tie it off.

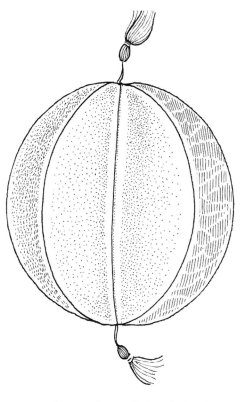

G. Tack a tassel to each dimpled end.

VICTORIAN-CHIC ROUND PILLOW
Combine luxurious fabrics and trims to make this ornate round pillow.

victorian-chic round pillow

By Dawn Anderson

SEW THIS HIGH-STYLE silk and tapestry pillow to augment an opulent decor or add a note of contrast to a modern interior. The circle medallion suggests hours of handwork and embroidery, but it's actually assembled by combining different fabrics and purchased trims. Since the fabric pieces are fairly small, try shopping for remnants of exquisite designer fabrics instead of buying off the bolt. The medallion is set off by a silk dupioni border that is shirred over a muslin circle for foolproof shaping.

materials

Makes one 16" round pillow

- 45"-wide fabrics:
  - ⅔ yard silk dupioni
  - ⅜ yard tapestry
  - ⅜ yard woven stripe
  - ½ yard muslin
- 2⅝ yards ⅛" rope welting
- 1⅛ yards tasseled fringe trim
- 1 yard ⅛" braid trim
- 2⅜ yards ¼" twill tape
- Thread to match fabrics
- Monofilament nylon thread
- 16" round pillow form

You'll also need: sewing machine, zipper foot, iron and ironing board, rotary cutter, clear acrylic grid ruler, self-healing cutting mat, sewing shears, pins, hand-sewing needle, compass with chalk pencil, large sheet of paper, and pencil.

instructions

1. **Cut decorative fabrics.** Cut four $5\frac{1}{2}$" x 41" silk dupioni strips (on crosswise grain); four 5" x 10" tapestry rectangles; and two $2\frac{3}{8}$" x 10" striped rectangles (center stripe design along strip length).

2. **Cut muslin circles.** Draft two perpendicular 17" lines to make a cross. Starting at midpoint, measure out 8" along one line and mark dot. Continue measuring from midpoint, marking dots 1" apart all around (illustration A). Cut along dotted outline for 16" circle pattern. Cut two 16" muslin circles; mark each edge in quarters.

3. **Sew two tapestry circles.** Right sides together, sew tapestry to striped rectangle along 10" edge, making $\frac{1}{2}$" seam. Join second tapestry to opposite edge so stripe is centered. On right side, using monofilament thread, zigzag flat braid over seams (illustration B). Draft and cut $8\frac{1}{2}$"-diameter circle, centered, from entire piece. Pin rope welting to outer edge; machine-baste using zipper foot. Turn under raw edge. Repeat to make a second circle.

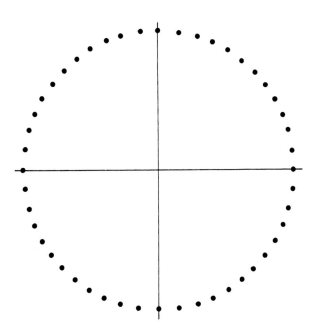

A. Mark dots 8" from intersection of perpendicular lines to make a 16"-diameter circle.

B. Sew tapestry to each side of striped rectangle. Zigzag flat braid over seams.

4. Complete pillow front and back. Sew two silk dupioni strips together at short ends to make large loop. Machine-baste ¼" and ½" in from each long edge all around. Pin-mark each edge in quarters. Draw up gathering stitches along both edges to make doughnut. Pin doughnut to muslin circle, matching quarter marks at outer edge; adjust gathers evenly (illustration C). Baste between gathering rows. Center and pin tapestry circle on top. Stitch in rope welting ditch through all layers to make pillow front (illustration D). Repeat for pillow back.

5. Assemble pillow. Cut twill tape equal to circumference of pillow form plus 1". Overlap ends 1", stitch together, and mark loop in quarters. Machine-baste pillow front ⅜" from raw edge all around; make quarter marks. Pin twill tape to edge, gathering pillow front to match quarter marks, and stitch. Repeat for pillow back. Stitch welting around pillow front, and turn under. Pin welting edge over tasseled fringe, and stitch in ditch. Pin pillow back to form. Pin pillow front to form, overlapping edge of pillow back. Hand-stitch all around.

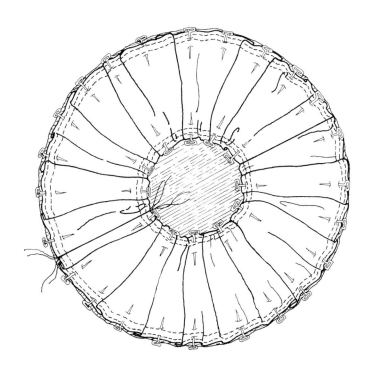

C. Pin gathered silk doughnut to muslin circle.

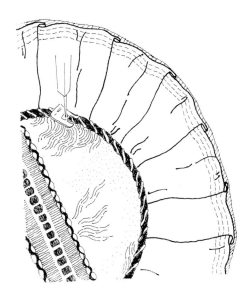

D. Sew tapestry circle to center of pillow by stitching in the ditch of rope welting.

PYRAMID-SHAPED PILLOWS

For variation, make each side from coordinating shades of velvet.

pyramid-shaped pillows

LOOKING FOR A unique and stylish pillow for your bed or sofa? This pyramid-shaped pillow, made here from rich colors of cotton velveteen, works up quickly and easily.

The form I selected, which measures 14", is filled with feathers and down for especially sumptous loft. Pyramid forms are available in many sizes, from 14" to 34" (see "Sources," page 96).

For finishing touches, consider adding tassels at each corner, embroidered crests and patches, or designer buttons. You can also enclose trims such as moss fringe in the seams.

materials

Makes one 12"-high pillow

- ½ yard 45"-wide cotton velveteen
- 14" three-dimensional triangle pillow form
- Matching thread

You'll also need: triangle pattern (see page 29), access to photocopier with enlarger, sewing machine, iron and ironing board, rotary cutter, clear acrylic grid ruler, self-healing cutting mat, scissors, hand-sewing needle, pins, and point turner.

instructions

1. **Cut four velveteen triangles.** Photocopy pattern (page 29), enlarging it by 400%. Lay velveteen fabric right side up on cutting mat. Determine fabric nap direction, then pin pattern to fabric to correspond. Cut out triangle using rotary cutter and acrylic grid ruler; mark XX edge with pin. Repeat process to cut three triangles total for pillow sides. Cut a fourth triangle in same way, except turn pattern 180° so

nap runs in opposite direction from arrow; mark XX edge with pin. Set fourth triangle (with nap running in opposite direction) aside for pillow base.

2. Sew three pillow sides. Place two "side" triangles right sides together and edges matching. Machine-stitch from X to Y along one edge only, backtacking at beginning and end (illustration A). Flip top triangle back on itself to expose triangle underneath. Place third side triangle on exposed edge, right sides together, and stitch from X to Y as before. Finally, sew two remaining free edges together from X to Y. Press seams open.

3. Join pillow base. Align XX edge of pillow base and one pillow side, right sides together. Stitch from X to X, backtacking at beginning and end. Pin one XY base edge to XX side edge, then stitch between dots on pattern, easing to fit. To join final edges, pin them right sides together, then stitch from each dot for 1½", backtacking at beginning and end; leave 11" middle section open for turning (illustration B). Press seams open.

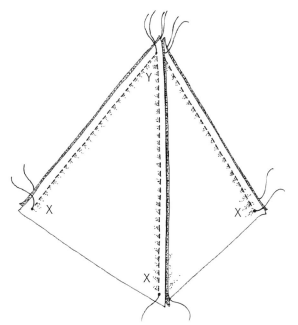

A. Join three triangles along the XY edges.

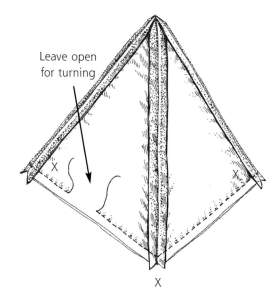

B. Join the base triangle, leaving an opening for turning.

4. Enclose pillow form in cover. Using scissors, clip off points of pillow cover diagonally at corners. Trim all seam allowances (except at opening) to ¼"; taper to ⅛" near points. Turn right side out and poke out points with point turner. Compress pillow form, insert into cover, and adjust fit at points. Pin opening closed, then slipstitch with matching thread (illustration C).

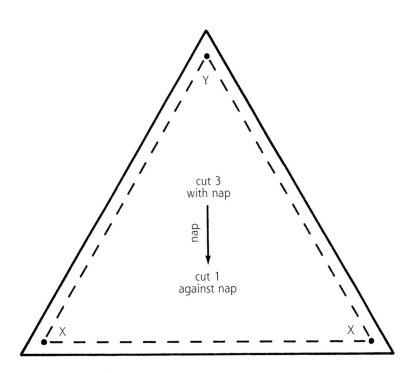

C. Insert the pillow form in the cover and slipstitch closed.

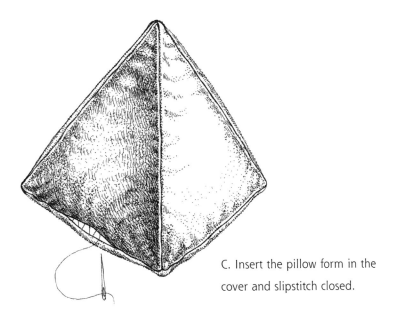

Pyramid-Shaped Pillow Pattern. Photocopy at 400%.

PRIMITIVE-PRINT PILLOW
Use bleach to create the look of
African mudcloth prints.

primitive-print pillow

By Nancy Worrell

AFRICAN MUDCLOTH DESIGNS are outlined by hand and colored with mud-fermented dyes. I mimicked the look using ordinary household bleach. The lighter area in each print is where the color was bleached out. To make the dot pattern, I dabbed on the bleach solution with a cotton swab. For the zebra stripes, I used torn strips of tape as a mask and applied the bleach solution with a spray bottle.

While the technique is easy, chlorine bleach is a potent chemical that should be used with care. I chose 100 percent cotton velveteen because the dense, plush surface seems to accept bleaching better than smooth, light-weight fabrics. Generally speaking, plant fibers are safe, but animal fibers such as wool and silk are too delicate. To neutralize the bleaching action, rinse the fabric in a weak solution of white vinegar and follow up with a thorough washing.

materials

Makes one 14"-square pillow

- 45"-wide 100% cotton velveteen:
    - ½ yard brown
    - ½ yard black
- 3 yards ½" black rope cordng
- Black sewing thread
- 14" pillow form

You'll also need: sewing machine, washer and dryer, iron and ironing board, liquid chlorine bleach, white vinegar, 5-gallon plastic basin (or utility sink), dishwashing gloves, safety goggles, small spray bottle, measuring cup, plastic drop cloth, 1"-wide masking tape, cotton swabs, rotary cutter, clear acrylic grid ruler, self-healing cutting mat, hand-sewing needle, velvet board, and chalk.

instructions

1. Prepare velveteens and work area. Prewash velveteens in mild detergent to remove sizing, and tumble dry. Cut black velveteen in half, parallel to selvage, and set one piece aside for pillow back. Choose a well-ventilated work area, preferably outdoors, and lay down plastic drop cloth. Fill basin with water and add ¼ cup vinegar. Fill spray bottle with equal amounts of liquid bleach and water.

➤ Designer's Tip

Chlorine bleach is a chemical, so use it with caution. Read the bottle label and follow the manufacturer's safety precautions. Wear rubber gloves, safety goggles, and old clothing. Before treating any fabric with bleach, prewash it in hot water with a mild detergent. Chemicals on the fabric, such as sizing, could react with the bleach to produce toxic fumes. Work in a well-ventilated area, preferably outdoors, and protect the area under your fabrics with a plastic drop cloth.

2. Bleach "zebra" stripes. Tear masking tape lengthwise, so edges are jagged, and apply to right side of black velveteen in a striped pattern. Put on gloves and goggles. Spray bleach solution lightly over surface; to prevent bleeding, do not saturate. Monitor closely; untaped areas should begin fading within a few minutes. To halt bleaching, rinse velvet immediately in vinegar water. Do not let fabric fold over onto itself.

3. Bleach dot pattern. Using chalk, sketch zigzagging diamonds (or another linear design) on right side of brown velveteen. Dip cotton swab in bleach solution and touch it to fabric in a series of dots along chalk lines; remoisten or replace swab as needed. Rinse as in step 2. Machine-wash and -dry both velveteens.

4. Assemble pillow. Machine-stitch bleached velveteens together along one edge; press seam open over a velvet board. For pillow front, cut one black/brown 14½" square, offsetting the seam (see photo, page 30). Cut one 14½" square from reserved black fabric for pillow back. Stitch squares, right sides together, ½" from edges, leaving 10" opening on one edge. Turn right side out, insert pillow form, and hand-sew opening closed. Tack 25" length of black cord to each seamed edge. Knot ends together at each corner, and fluff out excess (illustration A).

A. Tie ends of cord in a knot at corners. Unravel ends to fray.

➤ Designer's Tip

Use this bleaching technique to create contemporary-looking pillows. Place a masking-tape resist over the velveteen fabric in a checkerboard or striped pattern. Spray the fabric with bleach solution to create a pattern of bleached squares or straight lines. To create more interest, try varying the width of each line. For large polka dots, use a sponge dauber, available at rubber-stamping stores, to apply the bleach solution. Omit the rope cording for a stylishly simple look.

SARI TABLE RUNNER

Brighten your table with opulent silk fabrics embellished with shimmering beads.

sari table runner

By Dawn Anderson

USE THIS SILK RUNNER in any number of ways: on a table top or buffet, draped lengthwise over the back of a sofa, or as a vertical hanging on a wall or a door. The runner is assembled with border strips sewn around a center panel. Here, the border strips are cut from authentic Indian sari silk. Many large cities have sari fabric shops that cater to an immigrant population. However, if it isn't possible for you to see these beautiful fabrics in person, you can always purchase them through mail-order sources (see "Sources," page 96).

The center panel, cut from silk dupioni, is decorated with flat-backed beads that are hand-sewn in place. These beads mimic the reflective shisha mirrors often used in Indian textiles. I chose iridescent bronze beads for a subtle glimmer against the olive background, but you might prefer brighter silver or gold beads, depending on the color of your background silk. With care, the beads can also be glued in place with a "gem" glue, but test a sample swatch first to make certain you like the effect.

materials

Makes one 18" x 58" runner

- 1 yard 54"- to 60"-wide silk sari fabric
- 1¾ yards 45"-wide silk dupioni
- 1 yard Fusi-Knit interfacing
- 63 vintage flat-back beads
- Thread to match fabrics
- Beading thread

You'll also need: sewing machine, iron and ironing board, rotary cutter, clear acrylic grid ruler, self-healing cutting mat, chalk pencil, sewing shears, beading needle, hand-sewing needle, and pins.

instructions

1. Cut fabrics. From sari silk, cut two 5" x 51" and two 5" x 19" border strips (plan cuts so designs are aligned, if possible). From silk dupioni, cut 19" x 59" lining and 11" x 51" center panel. From interfacing, cut 11" x 51" rectangle; fuse to wrong side of center panel, following manufacturer's instructions.

2. Sew borders to center panel. Pin longer border strips to each side of center panel, right sides together. Stitch ½" from edges. Press seams open (illustration A). Sew shorter border strips to each end. Entire piece should measure 19" x 59" (illustration B).

3. Mark center panel. Using chalk pencil, lightly draft 8" x 48" rectangle on center panel by measuring 1" in from seam all around. Starting at one corner, mark dots 4" apart all the way around. Draft diagonal line connecting two dots closest to corner. Draft parallel line connecting next two dots (illustration C). Continue in this way until you reach the opposite diagonal corner. Repeat from other direction to mark intersecting diamonds.

4. Sew beads to center panel. Thread beading needle with beading thread. Sew one bead at each corner, dot, or diamond intersection (three beads in end row, two in second row, three in third row, etc.) until entire panel is beaded (illustration D). Brush away chalk marks.

5. Add lining. Pin beaded runner to lining, right sides together. Stitch ½" from edge all around, leaving 8" opening on one short edge for turning. Clip corners. Turn right side out, push out corners, and press well. Slipstitch opening closed.

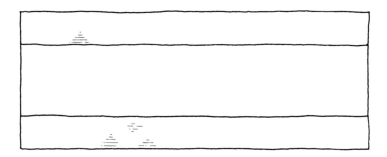

A. Sew long side border strips to center panel.

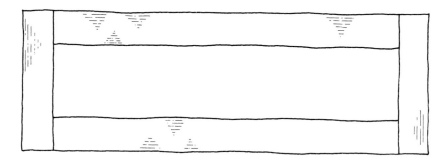

B. Sew short border strips to ends of center panel.

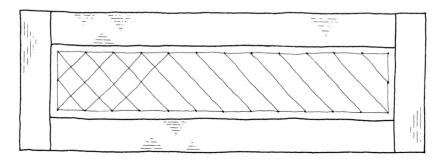

C. Draw parallel diagonal lines to connect dots.

Repeat in other direction.

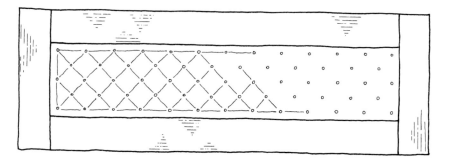

D. Sew beads at corners, dots, and line intersections.

HOLIDAY TABLE WRAP

Dress up your holiday table with this fast-and-easy,
crinkled-organza table collar.

holiday table wrap

By Dawn Anderson

TRY THIS FAST yet elegant way to transform your holiday table. This table collar, made from crinkled metallic organza, measures about 5¾" long, and double-sided tape secures it to the edge of a tablecloth. Always secure the collar over a tablecloth, since attaching it directly to the table could mar the finish.

To get started, measure the circumference or perimeter of the table. Note that one width of fabric after gathering measures about 24" long. To determine fabric yardage, divide the circumference measurement of the table by 24, then multiply by 6½" (the cut length of the collar) and divide by 36 to find the yardage.

materials

Makes one table collar

- Crinkled metallic organza
- Ribbon, 1" wide (MOKUBA #4568, amount equal to circumference of table, plus 2")
- 34-gauge spool wire
- Thread to match fabric

You'll also need: sewing machine, pin-tuck foot attachment, sewing shears, pins, ruler, newsprint, clear nail polish, and double-sided tape.

instructions

1. **Measure and cut the collar pieces.** Make clip along selvage at one end of fabric. Tear across the width of the fabric to make a straight edge. Measure the circumference of the table and divide by 24 to determine the number of fabric widths needed. Make clips 6½" apart along the selvage for the number of fabric widths needed. Tear across the width of the fabric at each clip mark. Trim off the selvages at the sides of each strip.

2. **Stitch the strips together.** Pin strips right sides together along short sides. Stitch ⅜" from raw edges; zigzag close to stitching within seam allowances. Trim close to zigzag stitching. Finger-press seam allowances to one side. Repeat to stitch all widths of fabric together.

3. **Stitch wire to lower edge of collar.** Fold up ⅜" of fabric to wrong side and finger-press. Attach pin-tuck foot to sewing machine. Position 34-gauge wire in the crease of the ⅜" fold, and set machine to a medium-width zigzag stitch, with a stitch length of about 15 stitches per inch. With wrong side up, zigzag along edge of fold, encasing wire (illustration A).

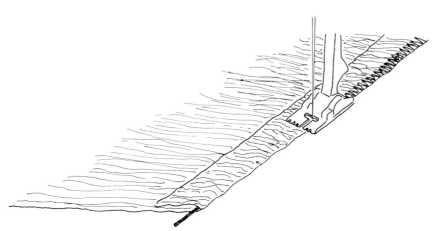

A. Encase wire in fold of fabric with a zigzag stitch.

Hold the wire from behind for the first couple of inches. Then hold wire from in front of the needle, pulling slightly to the right to keep it in the crease. Stitch for a couple of inches at a time, then stop to reposition wire and ⅜" fold. Continue in this manner until wire is stitched the entire length of fabric strip. Trim excess wire at ends.

4. Gather upper edge and attach ribbon facing. Stitch ½" from long edge opposite wired edge, pressing finger against back of presser foot while stitching to gather fabric slightly. Stitch for a couple of inches; release fabric behind presser foot, then continue until the entire edge is gathered. This is the upper edge of the table collar. Position ribbon on right side of table collar along upper edge, with one long edge of ribbon just overlapping gathering stitches, and short ends of ribbon extending 1" beyond the short edges of the table collar; pin. Stitch ribbon in place, stitching close to edge (illustration B).

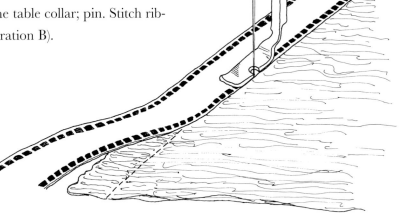

B. Stitch ribbon along upper edge of table collar.

5. Finishing. Trim seam allowances close to stitching along upper and lower edges. Protect work surface with newsprint. Apply clear nail polish to short ends of table collar and short ends of ribbon; allow to dry. Press ribbon to wrong side of table collar at one end.

6. Attach collar to table. Apply double-stick tape to back of ribbon. Press ribbon to edge of table to hold in place. Overlap ribbon at ends.

➤ Designer's Tip

To eliminate raw edges on seam allowances, join fabric widths with French seams. Pin fabric widths wrong sides together and stitch ¼" seams. Trim seam allowances to ⅛", then fold pieces right sides together and stitch ¼" from folded edge.

bed linen for a wedding trousseau

By Genevieve A. Sterbenz

THERE IS NOTHING more romantic than dressing a bed in heirloom linen. While usually expensive to buy, elegant bed linen is easy to make for a lot less money. The secret to replicating the look of beautiful linen worthy of a bride's trousseau is to buy good-quality cotton sheets and to decorate them yourself, using coordinated trims in different textures and widths.

The visual effect of combining ribbons and trims, all in white, is sophisticated and stylish. I calculated that I needed enough of each ribbon and trim to span the width of the sheet. And when I figured out my yardage for the pillowcases, I had to buy enough to go around the front and back of the case, as well as to multiply that measurement by two, since I was decorating two pillowcases.

When I laid out the decorations, it was clear that I would need to consider the fact that the pillowcases had only one seam into which I could slip the ends of the decoration. This required that I open the seam first. A second discovery was that I needed to stabilize the ribbons and trims first before I sewed them using a sewing machine since the ribbon slid around when I omitted this step. To achieve straight rows of decoration and to guarantee professional results, I applied scant dabs of fabric glue to the backs of the ribbons and trims, laying down the decorations on the sheet before sewing them. I also found out that to avoid twisting and buckling, I had to sew each row of decoration in one direction. That is, I began each row of stitching from the same side of the sheet or pillowcase, sewing top to bottom, top to bottom. These few hints should help you create a set of linens you will be proud to give any bride-to-be.

materials

For one queen-size flat sheet and two standard pillowcases

- 1 queen-size flat sheet in white (Barons Check by Waterford Linens)
- 2 standard pillowcases in white (Barons Check by Waterford Linens)
- 5 yards ¼"-wide polyester grosgrain ribbon in white (MOKUBA)
- 5 yards ⅝"-wide jacquard polka-dot ribbon in white (MOKUBA)
- 5 yards rosebud trimming braid in ivory (MOKUBA)
- White fabric glue
- Thread to match fabrics and trim

You'll also need: sewing machine, sewing shears, iron and ironing board, seam ripper, and tape measure.

instructions

EMBELLISHING THE PILLOWCASES

1. Prepare pillowcases. Press each pillowcase flat with iron set to appropriate fabric setting. Turn pillowcase wrong side out. Use seam ripper to open 2½"-length of seam beginning at open end of pillowcase and moving up. Turn pillowcase right side out. Position pillowcase horizontally on protected work surface with open end at left and ripped seam at bottom. Measure and mark four points along bottom edge beginning at left edge as follows: one point at 1", a second at 1⅝", a third at 1⅞", and a fourth at 2⅛", using straight pins. (Pierce top layer of fabric only.) Repeat process to mark four points on top edge. Turn pillowcase to other side and repeat process to measure and mark four points at both top and bottom edges. Turn pillowcase to front side.

2. Position ribbons. Measure and cut 42"-length of each trim. Set grosgrain ribbon and rosebud trim aside. Beginning at bottom edge, and leaving ½" overlap at ripped seam, lay polka-dot ribbon vertically on front of pillowcase with right and left edges positioned between the pin marks 1" and 1⅝" from the open end of the pillowcase; pin so left edge of ribbon is 1" from fold at open end of pillowcase. Remove one to two pins, lift up ribbon, and apply tiny dabs of glue to wrong side. Press down ribbon on pillowcase in same position, smoothing flat. Repeat process until entire ribbon is adhered to front of pillowcase; let glue dry (illustration A).

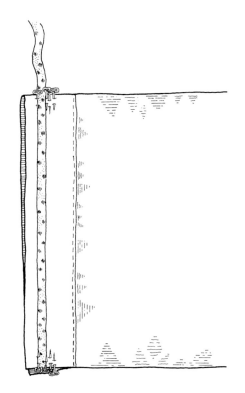

A. Glue-baste ribbon 1" from open end of pillowcase.

Repeat process to apply grosgrain ribbon to front of pillowcase, centering ribbon between third and fourth marked points on the bottom and top edges. Ribbon should run parallel to and be ¼" from right edge of polka-dot ribbon; let glue dry. Turn pillowcase over and apply ribbons to the back side in the same manner.

3. Sew ribbons and finish seam. Beginning at ripped seam, edgestitch one edge of full length of polka-dot ribbon to pillowcase. Repeat process to sew opposite edge of ribbon, beginning stitches at ripped seam and continuing for full length of ribbon. Stitch grosgrain ribbon to pillowcase in same manner. Turn pillowcase wrong side out. Machine stitch seam closed. Trim extra ribbon even with raw edge.

4. Add rosebud trim. Turn pillowcase right side out with seam at bottom edge and open end at left. Beginning at seam, center and pin right half of rosebud trim to open edge of pillowcase, allowing left half of trim to hang beyond fold and 1" to extend beyond seam (illustration B).

Continue to pin and glue trim to edge of pillowcase. At end, overlap one motif and pin; clip off extra trim and let glue dry. Beginning at seam, machine stitch trim to open edge of pillowcase continuing around and ending at overlap.

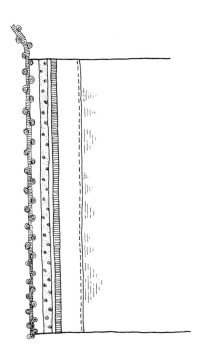

B. Apply rosebud trim to edge of open end of pillowcase.

Embellishing the Sheet

1. Prepare sheet. Press sheet flat with iron set to appropriate fabric setting. Place sheet onto work surface so top hem is horizontal and within reach. Measure and mark four points at right edge, measuring from folded edge of hem as follows: one point at 1", a second at 1⅝", a third at 1⅞", and a fourth at 2⅛", using straight pins. Repeat process across hem, measuring and pinning marks at 6" intervals, until reaching left-hand side.

2. Position trims. Measure and cut 92"-length of each trim. Set aside rosebud trim. Glue-baste ribbons to edge of sheet as for pillowcases, following the general directions in step 2 above. Cut end of polka-dot ribbon to ¼" overhang. Fold under ¼" to create hem that is flush with side of sheet; use dab of glue to secure to fabric. Repeat process to secure grosgrain ribbon. Pin rosebud trim to edge of sheet, allowing bottom half of trim to hang below fold; clip rosebud trim so end has one full motif. Glue-baste trim to edge of sheet.

3. Sew trims to sheet. Edgestitch along long edges of ribbons, making certain to sew all trims to sheet by stitching in one direction only. Machine stitch rosebud trim a scant ⅛" above center line.

SCALLOPED DUVET COVER AND SHAMS
Create a designer duvet cover and shams from flat sheets.

scalloped duvet cover and shams

By Amy Engman

I DESIGNED THIS duvet cover and shams to coordinate with the decor in my master bedroom. Rather than make the duvet cover from fabric yardage that would require seaming fabric widths together, I decided to make it from sheets. This option also allowed me to create a totally coordinated bedroom look because I was able to purchase additional matching sheets and pillowcases for making up the bed as well. I used one sheet color for the lower portion of the duvet cover and pillow shams and a second sheet color for the contrasting scalloped band. Purchased piping is inserted into the scalloped seam for additional detailing. The contrast flap covers the upper one-third of the duvet to ensure that it still shows after pillows are placed on top of it when the bed is made up.

I made an 8" facing along the scalloped edge of the contrast flap. This worked well since the two sheet colors I chose did not have a lot of contrast. If you are using sheet colors that contrast greatly, you may wish to face the entire contrast flap to avoid show-through of color on your flap. This is the method that I used for the pillow shams.

The contrasting scalloped flap is buttoned in place, using covered buttons. I purchased a button-cover kit and followed the directions for covering the buttons. I used scraps of leftover sheet fabric to cover the buttons, in order to get the buttons to match the duvet perfectly.

The instructions that follow are for a queen-size duvet cover with a 90" x 86" duvet insert. The finished pillow shams measure 20" x 30". To make a different-sized duvet cover or pillow sham, you will need to adjust the spacing of the scallops on the contrast flap. To do this, take the desired finished width of the duvet cover and divide by the number of desired scallops (use a number somewhere between six and eleven) to determine how far apart to space the scallops. Then reduce or enlarge the pattern on page 51 to the desired scallop measurement.

materials

Makes one queen-size duvet cover and two standard pillow shams

- 2 king-size flat sheets in primary color
- 1 king-size flat sheet in secondary color
- Covered-button kit for 10 buttons, 1" or larger
- 2 packages of piping to match sheets
- Thread to match fabrics

You'll also need: scallop pattern (page 51), sewing machine with zipper foot, rotary cutter, self-healing cutting mat, clear acrylic grid ruler, sewing shears, iron and ironing board, hand-sewing needle, and air-soluble marking pen.

instructions

MAKING THE DUVET COVER

1. Cut the fabrics. Cut a 91"-wide x 87"-long rectangle from one king-size sheet of primary color for the duvet cover back. Cut a 91"-wide x 66"-long rectangle from second king-size sheet of primary color for lower front of duvet cover. Cut a 91"-wide x 31"-long rectangle from secondary sheet color for contrast flap. Cut a 91"-wide x 8"-long rectangle from the secondary sheet color for the flap facing.

    Layer contrast flap and facing rectangles, aligning the lower long edges. Starting ½" from each side, mark scallop repeats 10" apart, 3½" from lower edge. Place pattern (page 51) on lower edges of rectangles between the first two marks; mark along scalloped edge of pattern, using air-soluble marking pen. Repeat across edge of contrast band and facing rectangles (illustration A); cut on marked line. You should have nine scallops across the width of the rectangles.

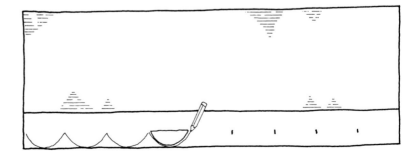

A. Mark scalloped lower edge on contrast band and facing.

2. Sew piping to scalloped edge. Pin piping, right sides together, to scalloped edge of contrast flap; clip lip of piping as necessary for a smooth fit. Clip piping lip at the inside point on each scallop. Using zipper foot, stitch piping in place (illustration B).

3. Stitch facings. Press up ½" to the wrong side of facing on the side opposite the scalloped edge. Press up ½" again to make a double-fold hem. Stitch close to inner fold. Pin facing to contrast flap, right sides together, along scalloped edge. Using zipper foot, stitch along scalloped edge, just inside previous stitches. Turn facing right side out to back of flap; press. Baste facing to flap along side edges, ⅜" from raw edges.

    Press ½" to the wrong side along the upper edge of the lower duvet cover panel, then press over 3" to the wrong side. Stitch close to the inner fold to create the facing for the lower duvet cover panel.

4. Make buttonholes, and cover and attach buttons. Cover buttons, using scraps of primary fabric, following the manufacturer's directions. Make machine buttonholes at the inner point of each scallop, positioning the lower edge of buttonholes 1" up from the scalloped edge. Make each buttonhole of appropriate length for button being used. On a large flat surface, lay out lower front panel of the duvet, facing edge on top. Lay the upper contrast panel over the lower panel, overlapping pieces by 6"; pin. Measure the length of the duvet cover top. It should measure 87" long. Mark button placement and stitch buttons to facing edge on lower duvet panel. Button contrast flap to lower duvet cover panel (illustration C).

B. Stitch piping to scalloped edge of contrast band.

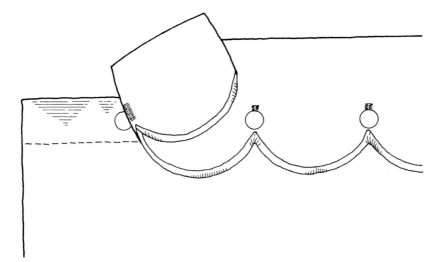

C. Button contrast flap to lower duvet cover panel.

5. Stitch the duvet cover. Pin duvet cover front to back, right sides together. Stitch ½" from all edges. Turn duvet cover right side out; press. Insert duvet into cover; button flap.

Making the Pillow Shams

1. Cut the fabrics. For each pillow sham, cut a 21" x 31" rectangle from leftover primary fabric for the pillow sham back. Cut a 24" x 31" rectangle from primary fabric for the lower panel of the pillow sham. From leftover contrast fabric, cut two rectangles, each 8" x 31". One piece will be used for the facing.

    Layer contrast flap and facing rectangles, aligning the lower long edges. Cut scallop design along lower edge of contrast flap and facing rectangles as in step 1 for the duvet cover on page 48. You should have three scallops across the width of the rectangles.

2. Attach piping and stitch facings. Follow step 2 on page 49 to attach piping to scalloped edge of contrast flap. Pin contrast flap to facing along scalloped edge, right sides together. Using zipper foot, stitch just inside previous stitching. Turn facing right side out to back side. Baste side edges together $\frac{3}{8}$" from raw edges.

    Press $\frac{1}{2}$" to the wrong side along the upper edge of the lower pillow-sham panel, and then press over 3" to the wrong side. Stitch close to the inner fold to create the facing for the lower pillow-sham panel.

3. Make buttonholes, and cover and attach buttons. Cover buttons, using scraps of primary fabric, following the manufacturer's directions. Make machine buttonholes at the inner point of each scallop, positioning the lower edge of buttonholes 1" up from the scalloped edge. Make buttonhole of appropriate length for button being used. On a large flat surface, lay out lower front panel of pillow sham, facing edge on top. Lay the upper contrast panel over the lower panel, overlapping pieces so entire sham measures 21" x 31"; pin contrast panel in place. Mark button placement and stitch buttons to facing edge on lower pillow-sham panel.

4. Stitch pillow sham. Pin pillow sham front to back, right sides together. Stitch $\frac{1}{2}$" from all edges. Turn right side out; press. Insert pillow form, and button flap.

Scallop Pattern

INVERTED PLEAT DRAPERY PANELS
Let these curtain panels add a casual
elegance to your room.

inverted pleat drapery panels

By Amy Engman

I USED SILK dupioni fabric for these panels because it has a rich luster and somewhat formal look, but it is relatively inexpensive. The inverted pleats are less formal than the pleating usually found in draperies, lending to a more casual feel. I did choose to line these draperies to prevent fading. The weight added by the lining also gives the panels a nice drape.

These panels are designed as stationary side panels to soften the window when used with a coordinating blind or shade for privacy. Since these draperies are stationary, only one width of fabric is needed for each panel. To achieve the widest panel possible, choose fabrics that are 54" wide. I usually hang my draperies about 3" above the window frame. I like my draperies to drag just slightly on the floor, so I make them a couple of inches too long to "break" at the floor. These draperies measure 86" long.

I used three monochromatic silk fabrics to make each panel. The colors graduate from lightest to darkest down the length of the panels. The top fabric section measures 10" long, the middle section measures 15" long, and the bottom section measures 61" long. To adjust the length of the draperies, simply add or subtract length from the bottom fabric section.

In general, space your pleats about 6" apart across the top of the panels and use about 6" of fabric to fold each inverted pleat. These measurements will vary slightly, depending on the width of your fabric. I actually used only 5¾" to fold the inverted pleats in these draperies.

materials

Makes one drapery panel

- Wood or metal pole of desired length
- Wood or metal rings to match pole
- 2 yards 54"-wide fabric in primary color
- ⅝ yard 54"-wide contrast fabric 1
- ⅝ yard 54"-wide contrast fabric 2
- 3 yards drapery lining
- Thread to match fabrics

You'll also need: sewing machine, blind hem foot attachment (optional), rotary cutter, self-healing cutting mat, clear acrylic grid ruler, sewing shears, iron and ironing board, and hand-sewing needle.

instructions

1. Determine finished length of drapery. Mount rod where desired. I mounted mine 3" above the window frame. Slip a ring onto the rod. Measure from the bottom of the ring to the floor and add 2" for the panel to "break" at the floor. Record measurement; my finished length measured 86".

2. Cut fabrics. Trim the selvages from the sides of the fabrics. Be sure to cut all three fabrics to the same finished width. For the top section of the panel, cut an 18½" length of fabric, with width equal to the width of the fabric. This allows for a 10" finished section, plus 8" for a 4" double-fold hem at the top and a ½" seam allowance at the bottom. For the middle section of the panel, cut a 16" length of fabric, with the width equal to the width of the fabric. This allows for a 15" finished section, plus ½" seam allowance at the top and at the bottom. For the bottom section of the panel, cut a length of fabric equal to the measurement determined in step 1 minus 10" for the top section, minus 15" for the middle section, plus 8" for a 4" double-fold hem at the bottom, plus ½" for a seam allowance at the top. The bottom section of my panel measured 69½" (86" - 10" - 15" + 8" + ½").

3. Sew drapery sections together. Pin top drapery section to middle section along the width of the fabrics. Stitch ½" from the raw edges. Press seam allowances open. Pin remaining side of middle drapery section to bottom drapery section along the width of the fabrics. Stitch ½" from raw edges. Press seam allowances open.

4. Hem drapery panel. Turn up 4" hem on lower edge of drapery panel; press. Turn up 4" again; press, and pin in place. Blind hem stitch by machine or hand-stitch in place (illustration A).

    Turn in 1½" side hem; press. Turn in 1½" again; press, but do not sew. Repeat for other side hem. Press up 4" double-fold hem at top of drapery panel as for bottom, but do not sew.

5. Prepare lining. Turn up 2" double-fold hem at lower edge of lining yardage. Machine stitch in place close to inner fold.

6. Line drapery. Place drapery panel wrong side up on a large flat surface. Open side and top hems of drapery panel that were pressed in place in step 4. Place drapery lining right side up on wrong side of drapery panel. Hem of lining should be 1" above bottom edge of drapery panel. Using inner press marks as a guide on top and side edges of drapery panel, trim away excess lining. Refold side hems, concealing raw edge of lining in hem; pin in place. Blind hem stitch side hems by machine or hand-stitch in place. Refold top hem on fold lines. Pin in place (illustration B). Topstitch ½" from upper edge of drapery panel, catching lining in the stitching.

A. Stitch a 4" double-fold hem at the lower edge of the drapery panel.

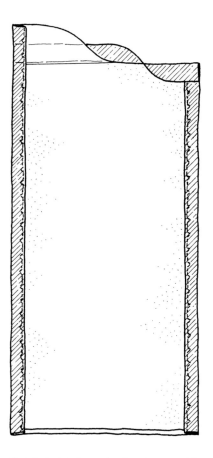

B. Stitch side hems by hand or machine, then fold top hem down.

> ➤ Designer's Tip

Silk dupioni fabric ravels easily. Handle the fabric carefully to prevent excess fraying.

7. Pleat upper edge of drapery panel. Pin-mark upper edge of panel 3" in from the side edges. Determine the number of pleats and spacing between pleats, using the chart below as a guide. (I used four pleats spaced 6" apart.) Mark upper edge of fabric with pin 6" in from first pin mark. Make inverted pleat, taking up $5\frac{3}{4}$" of fabric; use half of the fabric ($2\frac{7}{8}$") on each side of the pleat center. Pin in place. Repeat at 6" intervals. Topstitch pleats in place, stitching over previous stitching along upper edge of drapery (illustration C).

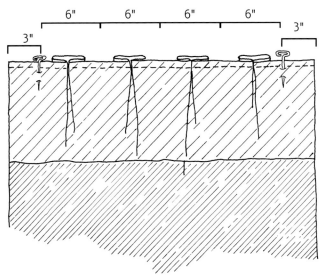

C. Pin pleats across top of drapery panel. Stitch in place.

pleat chart

Fabric width	54"	Space allowed between pleats	6"
Less fabric loss from trimming selvages	- 1"	Multiplied by number of spaces	
Equals cut fabric width	= 53"	(3 spaces between 4 pleats)	x 3
Less allowance for two side hems	- 6"	Equals total amount of space between pleats	= 18"
Equals finished width of panel	= 47"	Space available for pleating (from column 1)	- 41"
Less 3" allowed on each side before		Less total space between pleats	- 18"
start of pleats	- 6"	Equals amount left for pleats	= 23"
Equals space available for pleating	= 41"	Divided by number of pleats	÷ 4
		Equals amount for each pleat	= $5\frac{3}{4}$"

8. Hang drapery. Hand-sew rings to upper edge of the wrong side of drapery panel at center of each pleat. Sew a ring to each end of the drapery panel (illustration D). Thread rings onto rod, and hang drapery.

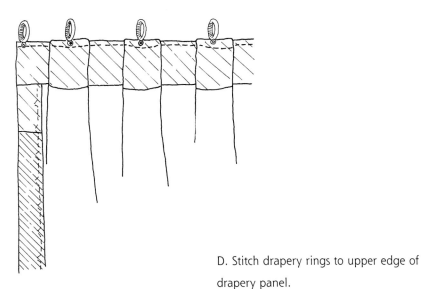

D. Stitch drapery rings to upper edge of drapery panel.

► Designer's Tip

Substitute clip-on rings for sew-on rings if desired. Clip-on rings are usually available in metal. See page 52 for inspiration.

BEADED FRINGE SWAG AND BEADED SWAG HOLDERS

Make a stunning swag in an afternoon from a rectangle of fabric.

beaded fringe swag and beaded swag holders

By Amy Engman

THIS SIMPLE SWAG from a rectangle of silk fabric has a self-fabric lining. The beaded detailing makes the treatment appear more complex than it is. I beaded the swag holders to match for a coordinating look.

For an attractive swag, I stretched a 17" length of fabric across the window and allowed for a 21" drop on each side of the window. Because my window was fairly wide, I decided to place two swags across the width of the window. To avoid seams in the finished swag, I cut the width of my swag along the selvages of the fabric. When the lengthwise grain of the fabric runs across the swag rather than up and down, it is called railroading the fabric.

To dress up the plain fabric rectangle, I decided to sew beaded fringe into the seam on the sides and lower edge. When stitching the beaded trim in place, use a zipper-foot attachment on your machine and be careful not to stitch over the beads, because you could easily break a needle.

For the swag holders, I started with unfinished wood holders. To prevent the wood from showing through the beaded embellishment, I painted the top of the holders with acrylic paint to match the beads. Be sure to use a wood primer on wood holders or a metal primer on metal holders before painting. For ease in decorating the holders, purchase your beads already prestrung. Seed beads are often sold in hanks that have several strands of prestrung beads knotted together. Be careful when removing a strand from the hank, since the beads can fall off the string.

materials

Makes one swag

- Fabric (amount determined in step 2 below)
- Round 2½"-diameter wood or metal swag holders
- Beaded fringe trim, 1" long (amount equal to determined finished length in step 2 below, plus 36")
- Seed beads on string
- White or clear craft glue
- Primer suitable for swag holder material
- Acrylic paint in color to match beads

You'll also need: sewing machine with zipper foot, rotary cutter, self-healing cutting mat, clear acrylic grid ruler, sewing shears, iron and ironing board, hand-sewing needle, and flat paintbrushes for paint and glue.

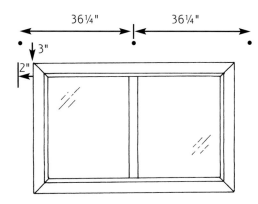

36¼" 36¼"

3"

2"

A. Mark location of swag holders on wall above window frame.

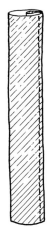

B. Make swag loops.

instructions

MAKING THE SWAG

1. Determine the number of swags and mark location of swag holders. Mark outside swag-holder locations on each side of window 3" above window frame and 2" to the outside of frame, using a pencil. Measure distance between outside swag holders. Swags should be spaced between 24" and 48" apart. If distance between swag holders is greater than 48", divide space evenly into desired number of swags. Mark additional swag-holder locations on wall between outside swag holders 3" above window frame (illustration A). I spaced my swag holders 36¼" apart.

2. Cut swag fabric. Measure the distance between swag holders and add 1" to the measurement. Multiply this measurement by the number of swags and add 21" twice for the drop on each side of the swag treatment, and then add 1" for two ½" seam allowances. I determined my fabric measurement as follows: Distance between swag holders equals 36¼" + 1" = 37¼" x 2 swags = 74½" + 21" for drop on one side +21" for drop on other side + 1" for seam allowances = 117½". Cut two 17"-wide rectangles from fabric to the determined finished length, cutting the length of the rectangles parallel to the selvages. I cut two 17" x 117½" rectangles.) One rectangle is for the swag and one is for the swag lining.

3. **Make fabric loops.** Wrap tape measure around swag-holder stem and add 1¾" to determine length of swag loops. Cut a strip of fabric 1½" wide by the determined length, for each swag holder. Press in ¼" on each long side of each loop strip. Fold strip in half, wrong sides together. Edgestitch close to edge with double fold (illustration B). Fold strip in half to make a loop; pin.

4. **Baste beaded fringe and fabric loops to swag front.** Place the swag fabric right side up on a flat surface. Pin loops to upper edge of swag fabric at locations corresponding to swag holders; match raw edges. Baste in place ⅜" from raw edges. Pin bead trim to side and lower edges of swag fabric. Hand-baste in place, and clip lip of trim at corners (illustration C).

5. **Sew swag.** Pin swag lining to swag fabric, right sides together. Stitch ½" from raw edges, using a zipper foot and taking care not to stitch over beads; leave a 10" opening on one side for turning. Turn fabrics right side out. Press gently, keeping beads away from iron. Slipstitch the opening closed.

   Fold swag fabric to make three ½" tucks, directly under each swag loop. Overlap tucks so only ⅛" of fabric is exposed for each. Hand- or machine-stitch in place (illustration D).

6. **Hang the swag.** Mount swag holders (see page 60) to the wall at the marked points, inserting swag loop on the stem of each hanger before mounting to wall. Arrange fabric drop on sides of swag into soft folds.

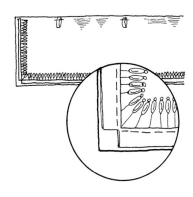

C. Baste swag loops and beaded fringe to swag panel.

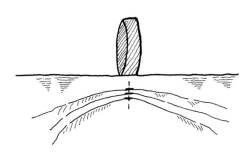

D. Make three tucks under each swag loop.

Making Swag Holders

1. **Paint the swag holder.** Prime the swag holder; let dry. Paint the swag holder with acrylic paint; let dry for at least 24 hours.

2. **Glue beads to swag holder.** Starting in the middle of the swag holder, gently brush on a small amount of glue. Carefully remove a strand of beads from the hank of beads. Starting in the center of the holder, secure the beads in a spiraling arrangement (illustration E).

   Continue spiraling beads around until end of strand is reached. Continue with additional strands in the same manner, adding more glue as necessary, until the beaded area measures about 1½" across. Switch to contrasting bead color and continue in same manner around front and sides of swag holder. Allow glue to dry for at least 24 hours.

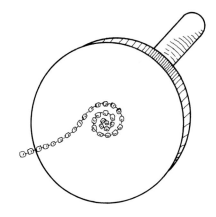

E. Glue beads to swag holder in a spiral.

FAUX-EMBROIDERED CURTAIN

Create the look of embroidery with easy-to-use transfer paper
and a colorful line-art leaf image.

faux-embroidered curtain

By Livia McRee

YOU CAN CREATE the look of embroidered curtain panels using a simple method of image transfer. The leaf transfers I used here can be found on page 65. I simply had the images photocopied onto transfer paper, cut them out, and then ironed them to my curtain panel in a random pattern. If you have a computer, scanner, and ink-jet printer, you can also use June Tailor Print 'n Press Iron-On Transfer Paper and still follow the directions on the following pages without making a trip to the photocopy center.

For stationary side curtain panels, make your curtain panels as wide as the width of your fabric. If you have large windows and want to be able to pull the panels closed across the window so they meet in the middle, you may need to piece additional widths of fabric together. A good rule of thumb for this kind of curtain panel is to measure the width of the window and divide by two (if you are hanging two panels, one on each side of the window). Then multiply this measurement by 150 percent and add 4" for hem allowances. This will give you the finished width to cut each panel.

Hang your curtain rod at the desired location. Measure beginning from about $1\frac{1}{4}$" below the rod to the desired finished length of the panels, and then add 4" for hem allowances. I have short windows and decided that my curtain panels should end a couple of inches below the window. If you have long windows, you may want the panels to end at the floor. You can also allow the panels to "break" at the floor by making them just a couple of inches too long.

The instructions that follow are for one curtain panel that measures 56" x 52" finished. If you are making a longer curtain, or more than one panel, you will need more fabric and more transfer images than indicated.

materials

Makes one 56" x 52" curtain panel

- Metal curtain rod
- Metal clip-on curtain rings
- 2 yards of 60"-wide lightweight white linen
- 3 pages of June Tailor Copy 'n Press Iron-On Transfer Paper for ink-jet copiers (1 pack)
- Leaf transfers (see page 65)
- White thread

You'll also need: paper, gluestick, craft knife or small sharp scissors, sewing machine, rotary cutter, self-healing cutting mat, clear acrylic grid ruler, sewing shears, iron and ironing board, and scissors.

instructions

A. Hem the four sides of the curtain panel.

1. **Prepare the transfers.** Color-copy the leaf transfers on page 65 six times. Using three pieces of white paper, cut out each image and glue down eight per page, using a glue stick. This will make 24 transfers, six of each image. Bring the three prepared sheets of artwork to a copy shop along with three pages of the June Tailor Copy 'n Press Iron-On Transfer Paper for ink-jet copiers (one pack). Be sure to bring the packaging so that the copy clerk will know how to handle the transfer paper.

2. **Make the curtain.** Machine-wash and dry the linen to preshrink it. Press the linen. Cut a rectangle to the desired length of the curtain, plus 4" for hems, by the width of the fabric; trim off selvages. (I cut my rectangle to 56" long x 60" wide.) Fold up 1" on the top and bottom edges of the curtain, press, and then fold them up another 1" and press again. Pin the hems close to the outer edges. Using a sewing machine, edgestitch along the inner folds. Hem the sides of the curtain in the same way (illustration A).

3. **Transfer the artwork.** Using a craft knife or small scissors such as those used for decoupage, cut out the leaves as close as you can to the outline, no more than ⅛" away from it, and closer if possible. Following the manufacturer's instructions, set your iron to a medium-high setting. Position an image with the printed side down on the curtain. Pressing

firmly, iron over the transfer in a circular motion for 20 seconds; gently peel one end up to see if the transfer is complete. If not, press the transfer back into place and keep ironing. When the transfer is complete, remove the paper immediately, while the paper is still hot, so that the transfer finish is more matte. (This makes it more difficult to see that the image is a transfer.) If the paper is allowed to cool before you remove it, the transfer will be shiny. Continue transferring the images in a random pattern over the curtain (illustration B).

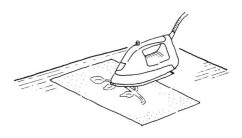

B. Transfer the artwork to the curtain.

Leaf Transfers

CHANDELIER DRESSING
Use a few beads, a chain, and some
fabric to accent a chandelier.

chandelier dressing

By Dawn Anderson

FOR A LAVISH accent, I wrapped this chandelier in sheer metallic organza and suspended glass beads from it to create an eye-catching focal point for any room. The crinkled texture of the fabric is created by machine washing and drying a plain-weave, metallic organza fabric. The plain-weave fabric shrinks substantially when washed. You could instead buy precrinkled metallic organza for this project to save on yardage, although the texture of the fabric would be more delicate than shown here. I wrapped the fabric around the arms of this chandelier twice; if you have a smaller fixture, you may wish to wrap it around the arms only once.

You can vary the number of beaded drops, depending on the size and style of your chandelier. Since this chandelier has five arms, I made ten beaded drops, two for each arm. I also made a set of drops to hang from the ball finial at the center.

materials

Makes one chandelier wrap

- Metallic organza fabric (amount determined in step 1 on page 68)
- 10 icicle beads
- 10 small bicone beads
- 5 large bicone beads
- 6 feet of 16-gauge brass wire; you will need more wire for chandeliers with large-diameter arms
- 6 mm gold chain
- 10 gold jump rings, size 6mm
- Thread to match fabric

You'll also need: washing machine, dryer, iron and ironing board, sewing machine, rotary cutter, self-healing cutting mat, clear acrylic grid ruler, sewing shears, straight pins, old bath towel, felt-tipped pen or wooden dowel that is slightly larger than arms of chandelier, wire cutter, chain-nose pliers, round-nose pliers, safety pins, paper, and pencil.

instructions

MAKING FABRIC WRAP

1. Determine fabric requirements. Drape a tape measure around arms of chandelier, wrapping tape measure around each arm and allowing it to drape between arms. Multiply measurement by 2 and record on paper. Wrap tape measure from cradle of one arm to top of fixture, spiraling it around chandelier a couple times. Add this measurement to previously recorded measurement to get finished length of needed fabric. Multiply finished length by .45, then add this number to the previous total and divide by two for the required fabric yardage. Round amount to the nearest one-eighth yard.

2. Prepare fabric. Trim selvages from fabric. Cut fabric in half lengthwise to make two long strips. Join the strips along one short side in a $\frac{1}{4}$" seam. Trim seam allowance to $\frac{1}{8}$". Fold fabric in half along seam, with seam allowances inside. Stitch a scant $\frac{1}{4}$" seam, encasing seam allowances in a French seam. Press seam allowance to one side. Press up $\frac{1}{4}$" on long edges. Turn up $\frac{1}{4}$" again and stitch close to first fold. Repeat to hem short sides.

3. Texturize fabric. Set washing machine on gentle cycle, and fill machine with cold water. Add fabric to water. Agitate for $2\frac{1}{2}$ minutes. Stop machine, and check fabric. For more texture, agitate further, checking at 30-second intervals. When fabric reaches desired texture, remove fabric. Roll fabric in old bath towel to remove excess water. Note that fabric dye may bleed onto towel. Place fabric in dryer and dry on medium heat until dry. Press fabric lightly with iron to soften and increase fabric width. Do not press flat.

4. Wrap chandelier with fabric. Wrap fabric around arms of chandelier, wrapping around each arm and allowing fabric to drape between arms. Conceal end of fabric between folds. Secure inconspicuously with safety pins, if necessary. Wrap fabric around chandelier a second time, allowing fabric to sit in cradle of arms; do not wrap fabric around each arm this time. At end, begin spiraling fabric to top of chandelier. Push end of fabric through loop at end of chain; secure with safety pins, if necessary.

MAKING BEAD AND CHAIN EMBELLISHMENT

1. **Make beaded hooks for arms of chandelier.** Make a loop at end of brass wire, using round-nose pliers. Close to loop, bend wire around a dowel or felt-tipped pen slightly larger than diameter of chandelier arm to make a hook for hanging. Trim wire about 1½" from hook (illustration A).

   Insert small bicone bead onto wire, pushing bead up to a point just below loop on hook. Trim wire to about ½" length under bead. Turn hook upside down; at top of bead, bend wire down at 90° angle. Insert end of wire in jaws of round-nose pliers and rotate pliers forward to make a ⅛" diameter loop (illustration B).

   Repeat to make total of ten hooks for the five arms of chandelier. Also make two hooks for center of chandelier, using large bicone beads in place of small ones.

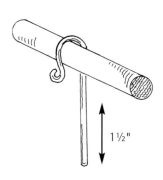

A. Bend wire around dowel to shape hook.

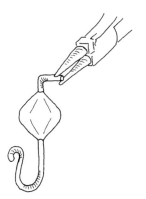

B. Make wire loop at end of bead.

> ## ➤ Designer's Tip

To create smooth wire loops with round-nose pliers, be sure to position the very end of the wire in the plier jaws.

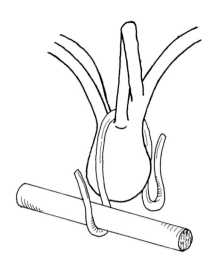

C. Shape double hook for center of chandelier.

D. Make wire loops at ends of center hook.

2. Make beaded hook for center of chandelier. Cut an 8" length of wire. Place center of wire over center of chandelier finial, and pull wire ends down around finial to shape the wire. Place dowel or felt-tipped pen used for shaping hooks at side of finial and push wire up over dowel to shape a hook; repeat on other side (illustration C).

Remove wire from chandelier. Determine end of hook, and cut wire ½" from desired end. Using round-nose pliers, make a loop on end of wire as before; repeat on other side (illustration D).

(Since my chandelier had five arms, an uneven number, my hook was made to fit on the chandelier so three of the arms are on one side of the hook and two of the arms are on the other side.)

3. Make beaded drops. Open loop at bottom of hook with small bicone bead, using chain-nose pliers; hook onto wire loop of icicle bead, and close loop with chain-nose pliers. Repeat for total of five drops. Repeat for two hooks with large bicone beads. Cut a 2" length of wire; make loop at one end as for loop at bottom of beaded hook. Insert large bicone bead onto wire; trim wire to ½", and make loop as before. Open loop at one end of bead and attach to loop at bottom of beaded hook; close loop. Open loop at remaining end, and attach to loop on icicle bead; close loop. Repeat to make total of five drops with both small and large bicone beads (illustration E).

4. Determine measurement for chain draped between arms of chandelier. Measure distance between centers of chandelier arms, using tape measure; allow tape measure to drape between arms. Separate chain into pieces of desired length (I used lengths of 8½"), using chain-nose pliers and flat-nose pliers to pry open links. Attach a jump ring to end of each chain length.

5. Attach chain to beaded drops. Open jump ring at end of chain; insert through loop under small bicone bead on a beaded drop having both a small and large bicone bead. At other end of chain, attach jump ring to a second beaded drop in the same manner. Repeat to link all five chains with the five beaded drops containing both small and large bicone beads; position all hooks to face in the same direction (illustration F).

6. Attach beaded drops to chandelier. Using hooks, hang beaded chain from arms of chandelier. Hang beaded drops with small bicone beads from each arm, hanging them at outside of beaded chain. Place center hook over finial and hang remaining two beaded drops from center hooks (illustration G).

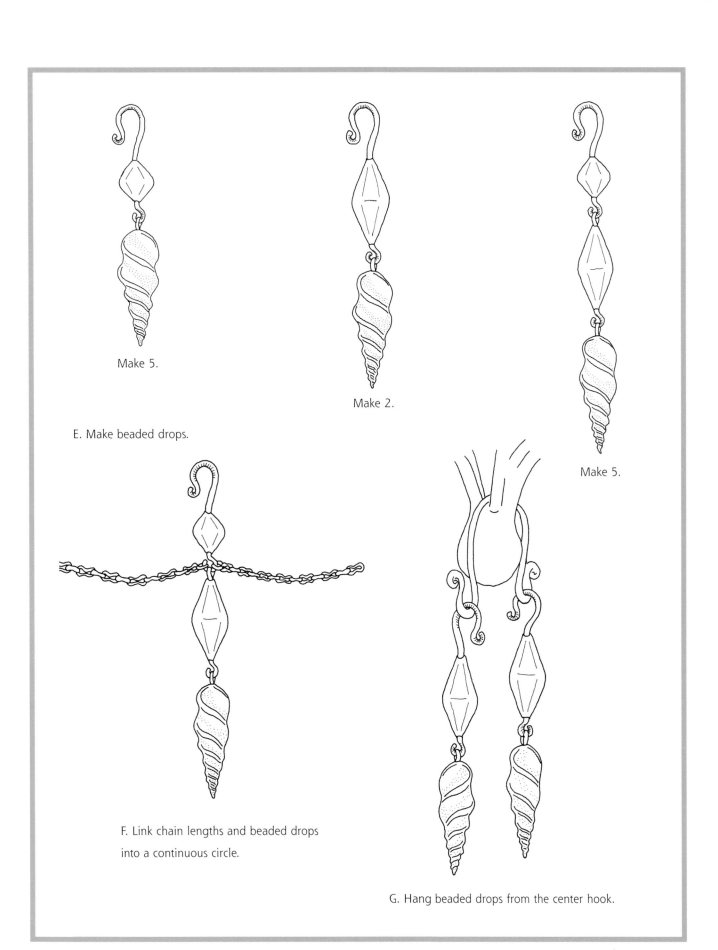

Make 5.

Make 2.

E. Make beaded drops.

Make 5.

F. Link chain lengths and beaded drops into a continuous circle.

G. Hang beaded drops from the center hook.

FABRIC-COVERED LAMPSHADE

Coordinate any shade to your furnishings with a little fabric and trim.

fabric-covered lampshade

By Genevieve A. Sterbenz

YOU CAN TRANSFORM an ordinary lampshade into a charming bedroom accent using leftover fabric and some pretty trim. If you have sewn other soft furnishings for your bedroom, you may have some extra fabric that you can use to coordinate a bed ensemble with this sweet bedside lamp.

I used a silk shantung in a bright checkerboard of lime and white for my lampshade. Not only do I love the color and pattern but I also like working with this fabric because it keeps its body and is lightweight enough to lie flat against the surface of the shade. The checkerboard pattern works on this lampshade even though the pattern doesn't match exactly at the back of a conical shade. I didn't mind because the lamp was going to be displayed on a small bedside table, and I could turn the lampshade to the wall so that the seam goes unnoticed. For a lampshade that is going to be viewed from all sides, choose a solid fabric, or one with an overall pattern.

To cover a shade you already have, you will need to learn a simple technique called laminating. All you do is apply a layer of fabric to a background surface, in this case, a lampshade, using glue. The join is so tight, you will think the shade was made from your fabric. The advantage of using a laminating technique is that you can cover any lampshade, as long as the shade is smooth and flat.

For added decoration, I accented the top and bottom edges of the laminated shade with cord in a coordinating color, and lengths of ribbon roses in an accent color.

The looped bottom fringe was made one loop at a time, in a process that is very easy. Wrap cord around a fat marking pen, and then secure the single loop with a few hand-sewn stitches. Repeat the process until you have a length of trim long enough to encircle the bottom edge of your shade.

materials

Makes one 4" x 8" x 7" lampshade

- ¾ yard silk shantung, 36"-wide, in lime-green-and-white check
- 4" x 8" x 7" conical lampshade in white
- 5¼ yards twisted cord in moss green (MOKUBA)
- 1½ yards rosebud floral ribbon tape in variegated crimson (MOKUBA)
- Cotton thread in moss green
- Yes Stikflat glue
- Bristle brush
- High-tack white glue

You'll also need: brown or white packaging paper for pattern, scissors, straight edge ruler, iron and ironing board, craft paper, tape measure, pencil, straight pins, hand-sewing needle, and fat marking pen.

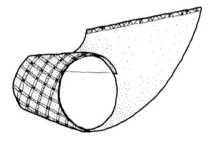

A. Center lampshade on fabric and smooth fabric around shade with hands.

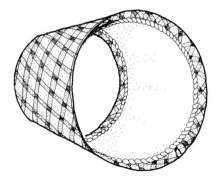

B. Glue cord over raw edges of fabric at inside top and bottom of shade.

instructions

1. **Make pattern and cut fabric.** Place lampshade seam side down on packaging paper. Mark paper at upper and lower edges of shade along seamline. Roll shade across paper, tracing upper and lower edges as you go, until seam is reached again. Again mark paper at upper and lower edges of shade along seamline. Remove shade. Connect upper and lower seamline marks at each end of pattern. Add ½" to upper and lower edges for foldover and ¼" to each end for overlap at seamline. Cut out pattern. Lay fabric on protected work surface. Lay pattern on fabric, rotating until desired orientation on fabric is achieved; use pins to secure. Cut around pattern, using scissors, then remove pins and lift off pattern. Fold over ¼" hem on right end; press flat with iron. Press remaining fabric; set aside.

2. **Laminate shade.** Use brush to apply thin, even coat of Yes Stikflat glue to all outside surfaces of lampshade, including top and bottom edges and inside lips, following manufacturer's directions. Lay fabric on protected work surface wrong side up. Center lampshade glue side down on center of fabric; lift and press left side of fabric to lampshade, smoothing flat, using hands (illustration A).

    Repeat process to adhere right side of fabric to lampshade; lap hem over raw edge, using extra dabs of glue to adhere. Fold and press top and bottom edges to inside lip. Set shade aside.

3. Conceal raw edges. Measure off 13¾" from one end of cord, and apply dab of white glue to cord at mark; measure off 25¾" from glued mark, applying additional dab of glue to cord at that measurement. Let glue dry. Cut cord at glued marks to make two lengths using measurements indicated in this step. (Glue prevents cord from raveling.) Where fabric overlaps shade onto inside lip at top, apply dabs of glue along raw edge of fabric. Beginning at seam of shade, position and press down one end of shorter length of cord, pressing cord around shade and ending at starting point; trim cord so ends meet, as necessary. Seal end with a dot of glue. Repeat process to glue longer cord to inside raw edge of fabric at bottom of shade (illustration B).

4. Trim top of shade. Measure and cut one 17½"-length of floral ribbon tape; set aside. Measure and cut two 14"-lengths of cord using the glue technique in step 3 to prevent raveling. Apply dabs of glue to outside top edge of shade. Beginning at seam of shade, position and press down one end of cord, going around shade and ending at starting point; trim cord so ends meet. Seal end with a dot of glue. Repeat process to apply second row of cord, just below first. Let glue dry.

   Measure and mark 2" increments around circumference of shade, starting at seam, directly below two rows of cord. Beginning at seam, position and glue rose at one end of tape to marked position at seam; secure with straight pin. Position and glue every other rose at mark at top of shade, gluing and pinning as before. Secure remaining alternating roses in lower position as shown, using dabs of glue. Let glue dry; remove pins (illustration C and photo, page 72).

5. Trim bottom of shade. Measure and cut 3⅛" yards of cord. Hold fat marking pen in one hand, and wrap cord around it to form loop. Slip loop off and use threaded needle to secure with tiny stitches. Snip thread, but do not cut cord. Repeat process to make loops until length of trim is approximately 26", or long enough to go around bottom of shade (illustration D).

   Invert shade and position on flat work surface. Run line of white glue around rim of shade. Beginning at seam, position and press one end of trim around shade. Loops will stand up. End at starting point; trim cord to fit, as necessary. Secure with pins. Let glue dry; remove pins.

   Measure and cut 26"-length of floral ribbon tape. Run white glue around front edge of shade at bottom. Position and press one rose at end of tape to seam. Secure with pin. Press tape down around shade and end at starting point, trimming to fit, as necessary (illustration E). Secure with pins. Let glue dry; remove pins.

C. Glue rose trim to upper edge of shade.

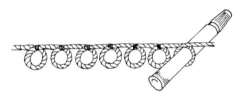

D. Make looped trim for lower edge of shade.

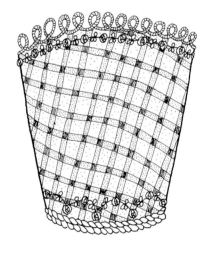

E. Secure floral ribbon tape around lower edge of shade.

CUSTOM "PRINTED" DIRECTOR'S CHAIR
Create the look of screened prints using a transfer
medium and photocopied art.

custom "printed" director's chair

By Nancy Overton

An ordinary director's chair can be transformed into designer seating by transferring an elegant print to a custom-made backrest. Since this photo-transfer technology is well suited to finely detailed artwork, I decided to transfer black-and-white engravings to my chairs. The technique is simple: The image you select is photocopied onto a sheet of photo-transfer paper, and then transferred to fabric with the heat of an iron.

I found these floral and ship engravings at the library. The shelves were full of collections of copyright-free engravings that are perfect for a project like this. You can use any color or black-and-white image; however, even for a black-and-white print, you must use a color laser copier to transfer the image to the transfer paper successfully.

My chair's original backrest was too coarse to produce a clear print and too heavy for my sewing machine. But I found I could easily create a new backrest—using the original one as a pattern—out of a muslin blend and cotton duck. The muslin let me achieve a clear, sharp print. Fusing the muslin to the duck adds durability and strength. The duck I used was a medium, 20-oz. weight made especially for deck chairs at 29" wide.

materials

- Director's chair (off-white canvas)
- ⅓ yard 45"-wide cotton/polyester muslin
- ¼ yard 29"-wide off-white cotton chair duck
- Fusible web
- Heavy-duty sewing thread

You'll also need: artwork for transfer (see step 1, page 78); photo-transfer paper; access to laser color copier; sewing machine with size 110/18 heavy-duty "denim" needle; Teflon-covered ironing board; iron; seam ripper; old, clean 100% cotton pillowcase; X-Acto knife; self-healing cutting mat; tracing paper; scissors; and pencil.

instructions

1. **Prepare pattern and select image.** Remove canvas backrest from deck chair. Pick out stitching with seam ripper, and lay canvas flat (illustration A). Iron out folds. Place canvas on tracing paper and trace around edges with pencil. Cut on marked line with scissors to make backrest pattern. To select image for backrest, look for copyright-free artwork (e.g., drawing, print, engraving) with a horizontal orientation and a length about two times the width. Size is not critical, since image can be enlarged on a photocopier.

2. **Photocopy image onto transfer paper.** Read transfer-paper instructions provided by manufacturer. Take instructions, transfer paper, artwork, and backrest pattern to copier center. Have artwork enlarged as necessary to fill tracing pattern, then have mirror image of artwork printed on transfer paper. Note that transfer paper prints on one side only and must be inserted correctly in the paper tray.

3. **Transfer image to muslin.** From muslin, cut rectangle about 2" larger all around than tracing pattern. Using X-Acto knife and cutting mat, trim transfer-paper image close to outline. To prepare iron, drain all water from it, preheat on hottest (linen) setting for 8 minutes, then gently shake back and forth horizontally to release remaining water droplets or steam. Turn steam feature off. Lay pillowcase on Teflon-covered ironing board, and smooth out wrinkles. Lay muslin rectangle on top. Press muslin with hot iron. Immediately, while muslin is still hot, center transfer facedown on it. Press lightly with iron for 20 seconds to initiate bond, then with heavy, even pressure move iron slowly back and forth across transfer for 1 minute. Make sure iron soleplate covers all parts of transfer, including edges. To remove transfer paper, rotate iron to reheat entire surface, then immediately peel up paper from one corner; if peeling is difficult, reheat and try peeling from a different corner.

4. **Fuse and sew backrest.** Lay backrest pattern on top of printed muslin with transferred image centered. Using fabric-marking pencil, trace pattern outline (illustration B). Cut out muslin backrest on marked line. Also mark and cut one backrest from canvas and one from fusible webbing. Following manufacturer's instructions, fuse muslin and canvas backrests together (illustration C). Fold long edges to back side using original backrest as a guide for hem depth. Fuse in place with thin strips of webbing or stitch down edges with machine. Fold in sides and stitch down to form channels for deck-chair stiles (illustration D).

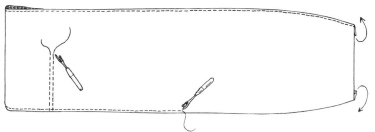

A. Use the chair's original backrest to draft the pattern.

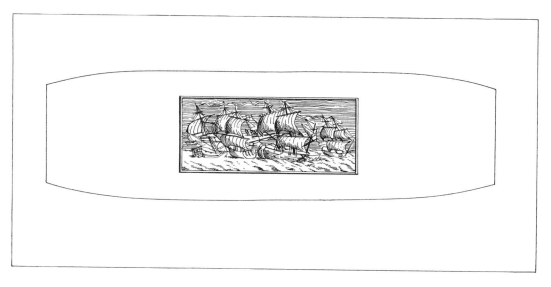

B. Transfer the pattern outline to the muslin, centering the image.

C. Fuse the muslin to a canvas
backing for added strength.

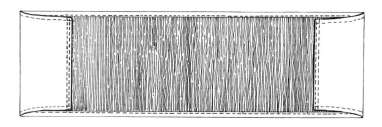

D. Stitch the side channels to match the original backrest.

PLAID SILK FOOTSTOOL

Create a small-scale footstool using a square of plywood for the base, foam for the loft, and curtain finials for the legs.

plaid silk footstool

By Francoise Hardy

YOU NEED ONLY basic woodworking skills to build this delicate footstool, which has a piece of plywood as its base and curtain finials for legs. If you can handle a handsaw, an electric drill, and a staple gun, you can build this 10"-high stool.

Because the stool has a smaller scale than, say, a sofa ottoman, I was able to take several design shortcuts. For the base, I started with a 14" square of plywood, then trimmed off the corners at a 45-degree angle to yield an octagon. This size piece of wood is easily handled with a handsaw, versus a larger piece of furniture, which might require a table saw.

Since the legs on this diminutive footstool are not going to support the full weight of an adult, they do not need to be as sturdily engineered as those on a larger ottoman, which someone might sit on. I selected a 6" turned maple curtain finial, which, when inverted, makes a beautiful leg. The legs are then attached to the base using hanger bolts and T-nuts, which are easy to work with.

The footstool's small scale also means there is no need for high-density foam. Instead, I used a 14" square block of ordinary foam, about 3" thick; the foam can be trimmed down easily using the stool's base as a template. To soften the edges and to make the final result look a little plumper, I applied a layer of polyester batting, followed by a layer of muslin, over the foam.

If the footstool were built on a larger scale, the bright, vibrant colors I selected would be overwhelming. The small size of this piece, however, means you can use just about any type or color of upholstery fabric. Best bets include bold geometrics in a medium scale, such as a plaid with blocks around 2" to 3". A large, 6" plaid would work better on a couch, while a tiny ½" plaid is better suited to clothing. Stripes can be difficult because they will wrap around the octagon in an odd way. I used a buffalo plaid, which lies in blocks of color and yet wraps around the octagon. (Naturally, if you change the color of the fabric from that shown here, be sure to change the paint colors to match.)

The top fabric is applied in the same way as the muslin: pulled taut on one side, then stapled in place. With the top fabric, however, I rolled over the cut edges and used a carded strip for a neat finish. Carded strips can be bought in rolls like tape, or you can make them yourself by cutting pieces of thin cardboard into ½"-wide strips. The strip is inserted in the fold of fabric before stapling in order to keep the edge straight and neat.

materials

Makes one 14" diameter footstool

- ¾ yard 45"-wide silk fabric
- 1⅜ yards 1"-wide tassel trim
- ¾ yard 45"-wide muslin
- 14" x 14" x 3" medium-density foam
- 22" x 22" polyester batting
- 1¼"-diameter cord-wrapped shank button
- ½" four-hole button
- Four 6"-long wood curtain finials
- 14" x 14" x ¾" piece plywood
- Four ¼" x 3" hanger bolts
- Four ¼" T-nuts
- Dental floss
- 2 ounces Plaid acrylic paint in the following colors:
    Fresh Foliage #954, Violet Pansy #440, and Crimson #435
- 2 ounces Plaid metallic acrylic paint in the following colors:
    Peridot #671 and Rose Shimmer #652
- Tulip Color Point Paintstitching, Pearl White #WH21
- Gold metallic felt-tip pen
- Water-based primer
- Thin cardboard

You'll also need: ½"- and 1"-wide soft-bristled brushes, 1" foam brush, staple gun, hot-glue gun, pliers, hammer, vise, drill with ¼" bit, handsaw, 100- and 120-grit sandpaper, sanding block, pencil, 20"-long ruler, T-square, scissors, 5" doll-making needle, scrap wood blocks, permanent marker, paper towels, masking tape, and serrated kitchen knife.

Other items, if necessary: four ½"-diameter or smaller furniture glides (for protecting bottom of legs).

instructions

BUILDING THE STOOL FRAME

1. Cut octagonal base. Lay 14" plywood square flat, smooth side up. Using ruler and pencil, lightly draft two diagonal lines connecting opposite corners. Measure from center intersection 7" along each of four lines and make mark. Using T-square, draft perpendicular line through each mark (illustration A). Resulting octagon will measure approximately 5¾" along each edge. Saw off corners on marked lines.

2. Drill holes for legs and button. Lay octagon flat, smooth side up. Draft two diagonal lines, perpendicular to each other, to connect opposite corners. At each corner, measure in 1½" and mark dot. Place scrap wood underneath during drilling to prevent splintering, then use ¼" bit to drill four holes at dots for legs and one hole at center intersection for button (illustration B). Drill completely through base into scrap wood. Sand surface lightly along woodgrain using 100-grit sandpaper in sanding block. To refine cut edges, run block against them at 45° angle.

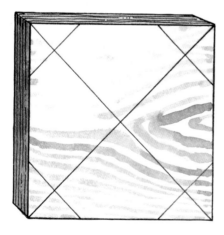

A. Draft an octagon on a square of plywood.

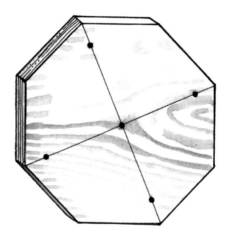

B. Saw off the corners and drill holes for the legs and the center tufting.

3. **Test-fit legs.** Position shank of T-nut over each leg hole, then tap in place with hammer until teeth embed and flanges lie flush with wood surface (illustration C). To add hanger bolts to finials, proceed as follows: Secure finial in vise. Using ¼" bit, drill 2" straight into center of leg. Using pliers, screw bolt into opening until just ¾" to 1" of bolt's threaded section remains visible (illustration D). Lay octagon flat, smooth side (stool underside) face up. To test-fit, screw legs into each opening from underside. Legs should lodge perpendicular to base, and stool should not wobble (illustration E).

C. Tap a T-nut into each leg hole.

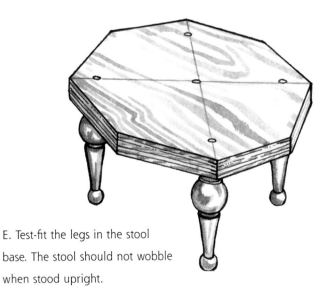

E. Test-fit the legs in the stool base. The stool should not wobble when stood upright.

D. Fit each leg with a hanger bolt.

PAINTING AND UPHOLSTERING THE STOOL

1. **Apply primer.** Start by making painting stand for legs. Using $\frac{1}{4}$" bit, drill four holes at least 4" apart and $\frac{1}{2}$" deep in scrap wood. Stand legs upside down in holes. Using 1" foam brush and following manufacturer's directions, apply one or two coats of primer to stool underside and four legs. Let dry overnight. Sand raised grain with 120-grit sandpaper and remove dust with damp paper towel.

2. **Paint stool underside.** Using 1" soft-bristled brush, apply three coats of Crimson paint to stool underside, letting dry 20 minutes after each coat. Note: Legs will be painted in step 7.

3. **Cut foam, batting, and fabrics.** Lay foam flat, set stool on top, and trace around edges with permanent marker. Using serrated knife, cut foam on marked lines. Screw in legs, stand stool upright, and place foam on top (illustration F). Drape batting over foam. Using scissors, trim batting even with top edge of plywood base and clip out small triangles to reduce bulk at corners (illustration G). To cut muslin, lay it flat, lay batting on top as a template, and cut 2" beyond batting edge all around. To cut silk, lay it flat, determine which part of design will fall at center of stool, and mark with small piece of masking tape. Fold batting into quarters and lay it on silk, placing folded corner at mark and aligning folded edges along lengthwise and crosswise grains of silk fabric. Carefully unfold batting, then cut silk 1" beyond batting edge.

4. **Attach upholstery.** Lay muslin flat, center batting and foam on it, and set stool base painted side up on foam. Unscrew and remove legs. Select muslin edge, cut along straight grain, draw it up onto underside of base, and staple it to center of side edge. Draw opposite edge taut but not tight and staple in same way. Apply several more staples along these two edges until you reach corners. Move two edges to right and repeat process. Staple remaining edges in same way. Screw in legs, turn stool right side up, and trim muslin even with bottom edge of base (illustration H).

F. Cut a foam octagon to match the stool base.

G. Layer batting over the foam, trim the batting and clip out the corners.

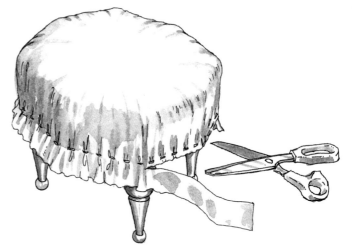

H. Staple muslin over the batting, then trim off the excess.

5. Add silk fabric covering. From thin cardboard, cut eight carding strips each measuring ½" x 5¾". Rest stool on flat surface, padded side up. Lay silk fabric on top face up, with tape marker at center and edges hanging down sides. Fold one straight-grain side edge under, even with lower edge of base. Slip carding strip inside fold to keep it even, then staple silk flat against lower edge, stopping 1" from corners. Repeat to staple opposite edge, pulling silk firm and taut. Move two edges to right and repeat process. Staple remaining edges in same way. To finish corners, pull fabric along one edge down and past corner (as if to make a hospital bed corner) and staple down. Tuck excess onto adjacent edge and make fold perpendicular to base. Repeat process at each corner, so folds "pinwheel" around octagon (illustration I). To further anchor fabric, place additional row of staples all around to secure any spots missed on first pass. Tap down protruding staples with hammer.

6. Add trim. Thread doll-making needle with 14" length of dental floss. Insert needle through hole in base of stool, up through foam, and draw out at center of silk fabric, removing tape marker as you go. Slip button shank onto floss, reinsert needle back down into cushion at center, and draw it out through hole. Thread floss ends through two holes in ½" button. Tie ends together in single knot, pulling snugly to create tuft on top of stool. Tie floss ends in square knot and snip ends. To conceal staples, hot-glue fringe around edge of base (illustration J).

I. Staple the plaid silk fabric to the stool frame, pleating each corner.

J. Tuft the center of the stool, then glue fringe around the edge.

7. Paint legs. Remove legs from stool. Use color silhouette, below, as reference for painting leg. Stand each leg on end so bolt rests on work surface, hold ½" brush against surface being painted, and rotate leg by ball foot. Allow 20 minutes' drying time after each coat. Paint middle ball element of each leg with two coats of Fresh Foliage, followed by two coats of Peridot. Paint flared cone with two coats of Violet Pansy. Paint convex collar with three coats of Rose Shimmer. Set leg in stand and paint ball foot and top disk with three coats of Rose Shimmer. Let dry 1 hour. Brush on acrylic gloss varnish, let dry 15 minutes, brush on second coat, and let dry 1 hour. To stripe rings, nest gold marker tip along crevice and rotate leg. Let dry 30 minutes. Squeeze dots of Pearl White fabric paint directly from applicator onto widest ring, spacing dots ¼" apart. Let dry overnight before screwing legs into stool. If desired, insert glides into bottom of ball feet following manufacturer's instructions.

RELAXED-FIT SLIPCOVER

The secret to making this baggy slipcover is to measure and cut the fabric against your chair and then stitch relaxed seams.

relaxed-fit slipcover

By Candie Frankel

A CUSTOM-MADE, LOOSE-FITTING slipcover like the one shown here might cost hundreds of dollars in an upholstery store, but with the right know-how, you can sew a professional-looking version in a weekend's time for less than half the cost, depending on the fabric.

Relaxed-fit slipcovers often look best when made from fabrics that have a washed, faded, or slightly crumpled look. Decorator fabrics made from cotton/linen or cotton/rayon will shrink and wrinkle slightly when washed, which contributes to the relaxed look.

To orient myself, I canvassed half a dozen home-decorating books that described methods of sewing slipcovers. One approach measured and cut pieces of muslin fabric against the chair to derive patterns, which were then used to cut the slipcover fabric. A second technique called for measuring and cutting the actual slipcover fabric against the chair, pin-fitting the cut pieces inside out, then proceeding straight to the sewing machine. The muslin pattern approach is ideal when you want to make more than one slipcover. The same pattern can be used to create a wardrobe of slipcovers for a single chair or a set of matching slipcovers for two or more identical chairs. For a single slipcover, however, measuring and cutting the fabric directly on the chair is a real time-saver.

My second important discovery involved seam lines and the way I created the relaxed fit. Instead of trying to introduce bagginess right off, I pin-fit each seam the traditional way for a snug fit, then ran a new line of pins three-quarters of an inch beyond the first line to mark the eventual seam line. This allowed better control of the fit, and prevented the final slipcover from crossing the visual border from baggy to outright sloppy. Rather than sew the pieces as pinned, I unpinned them first and proceeded section by section. This gave me the opportunity to trim symmetrical pieces and pairs, such as the front arms, so that their edges matched. In an earlier attempt, I skipped this step and produced some unattractive joins, particularly where the outside arm and inner and outer backs converged.

NOTE: *The yardage requirements and directions that follow are intended for solid-color fabrics or ones with small- to medium-scale prints that do not require meticulous matching.*

materials

- 54"-wide slipcover fabric (to calculate yardage, see "Getting Started," steps 1 through 3)
- ⅜" preshrunk cotton welting cord or purchased welting in contrasting color (to calculate yardage, see "Getting Started," step 2)
- Thread to match slipcover fabric
- 36" slipcover zipper (for cushion)

You'll also need: chair, sewing machine, 10 yards twill tape, T-pins, quilter's pins, tape measure, calculator, dark-colored chalk, scissors, iron, washer/dryer, pencil, and scrap paper.

Other items, if necessary: rotary cutter (to cut bias for welting); self-healing cutting mat; and clear acrylic grid ruler.

instructions

GETTING STARTED

1. Start by plotting slipcover seams. Wrap twill tape around chair shoulder, along outer arms, and around chair body even with deck (illustration A). To anchor tape, use T-pins: Pierce tape and upholstery, then pivot shank 180° and press down into upholstery.

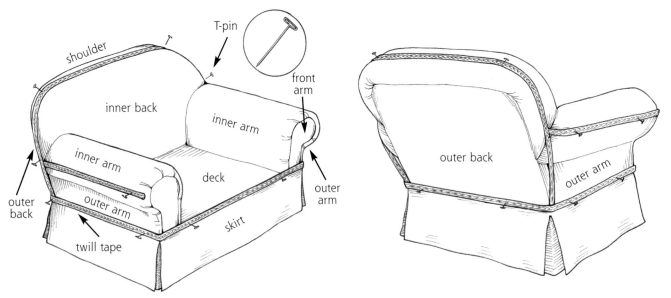

A. Anchor twill tape to the chair with T-pins to mark future slipcover seams.

2. Next, calculate welting yardage. Add (a) total twill tape measurement from step 1, page 90, (b) cushion perimeter times 2, and (c) 18" shrinkage allowance. If using purchased welting, eliminate shrinkage allowance. Jot down total.

3. Last, calculate fabric yardage. Remove cushion and measure chair front to back and side to side (illustration B). Measure floor to deck-level tape and multiply by 8. Measure cushion width front to back and add cushion depth times 3. Add all measurements and divide by 36". If making welting, add ½ yard per 10 yards welting (step 2, above). Add 1 yard fitting allowance. Add 8% of total for shrinkage. Jot down all measurements for future reference.

4. To preshrink fabric, machine-wash and -dry at medium setting.

BLOCKING THE SLIPCOVER

Shape the slipcover by pinning together rectangles of fabric that correspond to the chair sections (inner back, outer back, etc.; see illustration A). To provide pinning ease, cut each rectangle 3" larger all around than its corresponding chair section. To determine the appropriate dimensions, measure the fabric directly against a chair section. This measuring and cutting process is called blocking.

1. Begin blocking by folding fabric yardage lengthwise, wrong side out. Smooth it against inner back of chair so end of fabric extends 3" above shoulder tape and excess runs across deck. Make small chalk mark 3" beyond deck crevice. Fold fabric straight across at mark and cut along fold (illustration C).

2. Complete blocking first rectangle by unfolding cut piece from step 1 wrong side out. Lay it against inner back of chair, so one selvage extends 3" beyond shoulder at widest part. Mark fabric 3" beyond opposite shoulder. Fold and cut fabric at mark as in step 1 (illustration D). Set aside excess. Label section "inner back" and trim off remaining selvage.

3. To block rectangles for most remaining sections (outside back, inner and outer arms, and deck), repeat steps 1 and 2. For each piece, remember to mark fabric 3" beyond chair's widest point, to cut fabric straight across, and to label all pieces. Proceed section by section, top down, to cut one outer back, two inner arms, two outer arms, and one deck (illustration A). Set aside two large scraps for front arms, which will be added

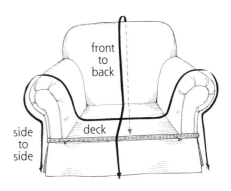

B. To determine fabric yardage, remove the cushion and measure the chair in two directions: side to side, and front to back.

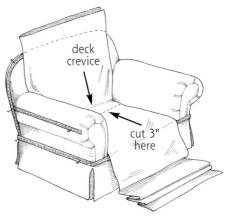

C. Begin blocking the inner back by laying folded yardage against the chair. Cut the fabric so 3" extends at the top and bottom.

D. Finish blocking the inner back by trimming the fabric so 3" extends at each side.

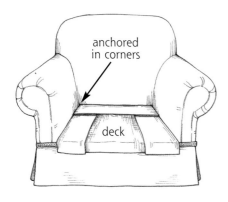

E. Fold back 3" extensions onto the deck to keep them neat during pinning.

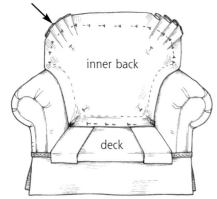

F. Anchor inner back piece, finger-pleating to ease the corners.

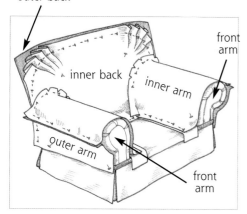

G. Anchor and pin the inner and outer arms.

in "Anchoring and Pin-Fitting," step 5. Remaining yardage will be used to cut skirt, welting, and cushion.

4. Measure cushion from front to back, add cushion depth times 3, and cut fabric to this measurement. For welting, cut fabric yardage calculated in "Getting Started," step 2, page 91. Reserve remaining fabric for skirt.

ANCHORING AND PIN-FITTING

In this set of steps, the rectangles and pieces are pinned together, then trimmed further to match the actual contours of the chair. Place the fabric on the chair wrong side out. Anchor the fabric to the chair's upholstery with T-pins, and pin-fit the pieces together using quilter's pins.

1. Start by anchoring deck. Lay fabric on chair deck and fold 3" extensions on three inner edges. Anchor four corners, leaving extensions free (illustration E).

2. Pin-fit shoulder seam by smoothing inner back piece across shoulder so edges extend 3" beyond chair. Anchor top and bottom. Anchor inner back piece so 3" extends onto deck. Pin this extension to folded deck extension. Finger-pleat inner back to ease corners (illustration F).

3. Pin inner and outer backs together at shoulder, following shoulder twill tape. Trim lower edge of outer back 1" below deck-level tape. Shape inner back piece by pressing it against (but not into) inner back and inner arm crevices. Let excess fabric fall against chair arm. Beginning at top of each crevice and working downwards, mark excess fabric 3" beyond crevice, resmoothing fabric as needed to create ease as you move around chair arm. Trim on marked lines (illustration F).

4. Pin arms by smoothing and anchoring outer and inner arms on chair arm. Inner arm should extend 3" onto deck. Trim lower edge of outer arm 1" below deck-level tape, even with outer back. Pin outer and inner arms together, along twill tape. Pin deck extensions together along straight edges, but angle pins towards outside deck corners for proper fit when skirt is joined. To ease inner arm, trim fabric 3" beyond inner arm and inner back crevices as in step 3. Starting at top of arm and continuing around curve down towards deck, pin seam allowances together 1" from inner arm and inner back crevices. Once edges straighten out, do not pin. To create ease, clip into fabric allowance, stopping just before pins. Trim ½" beyond pins. When you reach end of pins, angle cut down and out away from inner back/inner arm crevice. To complete join, pin-fit outer arms to outer back (illustration G).

5. To pin-fit front arms, anchor scrap fabric to each front arm so bottom edge falls 3" below deck-level tape. Pin-fit to outer and inner arm, following contours (illustration H).

6. Create characteristic bagginess by repinning all "twill tape" seams ¾" beyond existing pins, then removing first set of pins. Repin front arms to accommodate increased allowance. Adjust where arm and back meet. Remove anchoring T-pins. Try lifting slipcover off chair, arms first. If it is too tight, reposition pins along outer back/outer arm seams for more allowance. Trim excess fabric ½" beyond pins (illustration I).

7. With pinned slipcover on chair, notch seam allowances every 10". Remove all pins. To make sure pieces are symmetrical, fold in half or layer pairs, then trim corresponding edges to match. Repin pleats. If using purchased welting, proceed to step 1, page 95, "Sewing the Slipcover and Cushion Cover."

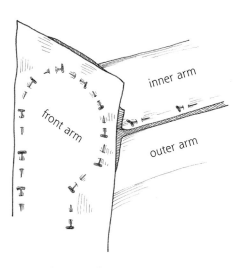

H. To form the front arm, pin reserved fabric to the inner and outer arms.

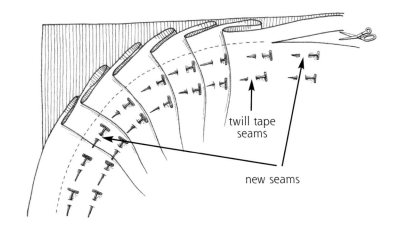

twill tape seams

new seams

I. To create characteristic bagginess, repin all "tape" seams ¾" beyond the existing pins and trim excess fabric ½" beyond the pins.

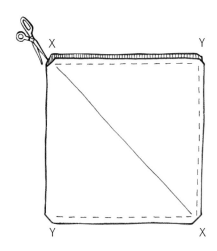

J. Determine the bias strip width by wrapping a small scrap of paper around the welting cord.

MAKING YOUR OWN WELTING

1. Wrap small section of scrap paper around welting cord, then trim $\frac{1}{2}$ away from cord (illustration J). Measure unfolded paper to determine width for bias strips.

2. Cut fabric yardage for welting, allowing $\frac{1}{2}$ yard of fabric for 10 yards of welting (see "Getting Started," steps 2 and 3, page 91). Fold fabric in half, sew edges together on three sides, and clip corners diagonally.

3. Label one corner and its diagonal opposite X. Label other two corners Y. Using chalk and ruler, draft diagonal line from X to X. Turn piece over and draft diagonal line from Y to Y. Using scissors, cut on each marked line through one layer only (illustration K).

4. Unfold and open cut piece; shape to form a tube and press seams open. Lay tube flat and trim raw edges straight. Use rotary cutter to cut strips to width determined in step 1, or use ruler and chalk to mark strips to width determined in step 1 and cut with scissors. Stop cutting 6" from one end (illustration L). Unfold and lay uncut section flat. To complete cuts, jog each cut by one strip width (illustration M).

5. Make welting by enclosing cord in strip, right side out and raw edges matching. Machine-baste using zipper foot.

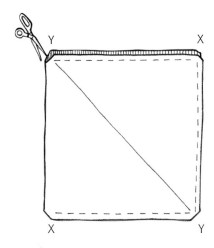

K. Mark two opposing diagonal lines, one on each side. Using scissors, cut on each marked line through one layer only.

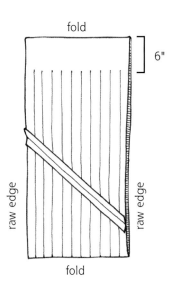

L. Lay the resulting tube flat, then cut parallel strips to the correct width, stopping 6" from one end.

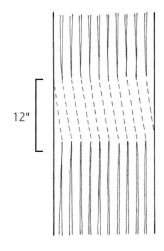

M. Lay the uncut section flat to complete the cuts, jogging each cut one strip.

Sewing the Slipcover and Cushion Cover

1. Join pieces by pinning and sewing right sides together, matching notches in the following order and enclosing welting in seams preceded by a W: Inner arms to deck; inner back to deck; inner arms to inner back; (W) inner arms to outer arms; (W) outer back to inner back/outer arms/inner arms; (W) front arms to inner arms/outer arms. Machine-baste welting ½" from lower edge of slipcover all around, butting ends for neat finish. Mark center of back, front, and sides of slipcover by notching; notches will be used to line up skirt.

2. To make self-lined skirt, place slipcover on chair, right side out. Measure from lower edge to floor, multiply by 2, add 1", and then cut four sections this length across fabric width. Sew short ends together in continuous loop; press seams open. Fold in half, wrong sides together and raw edges matching, and press. On raw edge, notch center of each panel (illustration N). Remove slipcover from chair. Match notches to center notches made in step 1, and pin from notches out to corners of slipcover; machine-stitch. To make inverted corner pleats, fold excess fabric evenly on each side of corner seam, then machine-stitch (illustrations O and P).

3. For cushion, start by making boxing strip. Cut one strip equal to cushion depth plus 1¼" across width of fabric. Anchor to cushion, leaving zipper section of cushion exposed. Cut second strip 1½" wider than first strip and 1" longer than exposed zipper section. Cut strip in half lengthwise and install zipper between halves. Sew strips together at short ends to make boxing strip. Test-fit on cushion, adjust as needed, and trim excess zipper tape. Cut remaining cushion fabric (from "Blocking the Slipcover," step 4, page 92) in half. Anchor each piece to cushion and pin-fit to boxing strip (illustration Q). Trim edges, then notch each edge at center. Disassemble, true up to make sure pieces are symmetrical, and sew as for slipcover, installing welting in seams.

4. When chair and cushion slipcovers are sewn, remove twill tape from chair. Ease slipcover on chair, right side out, and tuck deck extensions and inner back/inner arm seams into crevices. Put cushion slipcover on cushion and set cushion on chair deck.

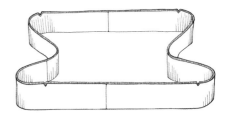

N. To make a self-lined skirt, join the skirt sections in a continuous loop.

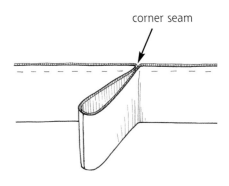

O. Sew the skirt to the sides, back, and front of the slipcover from the center out to the corners.

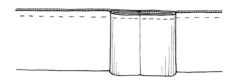

P. Fold the excess fabric flat and stitch it to form an inverted box pleat.

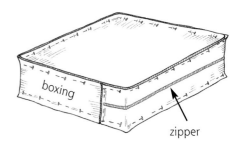

Q. Cover the cushion by cutting and pin-fitting the zippered boxing strip first. Then pin-fit the top and bottom fabric sections.

sources

Beads

Beads and Beyond
25 102nd Ave. NE
Bellevue, WA 98004
425-462-8992
Beads, wire

Fabrics

Super Silk, Inc.
PO Box 527596
Flushing, NY 11352
800-432-SILK
Silk dupioni, metallic organza

Pillow Forms

Down Decor
228 Townsend Street
San Francisco, CA 94107
800-966-1615

Wood Products

Rockler Woodworking
    and Hardware
4365 Willow Drive
Medina, MN 55340
800-279-4441
Wood finials

Contributors

Chinese Silk Pillows
DESIGNER: Dawn Anderson
ILLUSTRATOR: Jil Johänson
PHOTOGRAPHER: Carl Tremblay

Jewel-Tone Spiral Pillow
DESIGNER: Dawn Anderson
ILLUSTRATOR: Judy Love
PATTERN ILLUSTRATOR:
    Roberta Frauwirth
PHOTOGRAPHER: Carl Tremblay

Tasseled Ball Pillows
DESIGNER: Candie Frankel
ILLUSTRATOR: Mary Newell DePalma
PATTERN ILLUSTRATOR:
    Roberta Frauwirth
PHOTOGRAPHER: Carl Tremblay

Victorian-Chic Round Pillow
DESIGNER: Dawn Anderson
ILLUSTRATOR: Jil Johänson
PHOTOGRAPHER: Carl Tremblay

Pyramid-Shaped Pillows
DESIGNER: Dawn Anderson
ILLUSTRATOR: Judy Love
PATTERN ILLUSTRATOR:
    Roberta Frauwirth
PHOTOGRAPHER: Carl Tremblay

Primitive-Print Pillow
DESIGNER: Nancy Worrell
ILLUSTRATOR: Jil Johänson
PHOTOGRAPHER: Carl Tremblay

Sari Table Runner
DESIGNER: Dawn Anderson
ILLUSTRATOR: Jil Johänson
PHOTOGRAPHER: Carl Tremblay

Holiday Table Wrap
DESIGNER: Dawn Anderson
ILLUSTRATOR: Jil Johänson
PHOTOGRAPHER: Carl Tremblay

Bed Linen for a Wedding Trousseau
DESIGNER: Genevieve Stèrbenz
ILLUSTRATOR: Jil Johänson
PHOTOGRAPHER: Carl Tremblay

Scalloped Duvet Cover and Shams
DESIGNER: Amy Engman
ILLUSTRATOR: Jil Johänson
PHOTOGRAPHER: Carl Tremblay

Inverted Pleat Drapery Panels
DESIGNER: Amy Engman
ILLUSTRATOR: Jil Johänson
PHOTOGRAPHER: Carl Tremblay

**Beaded Fringe Swag and
Beaded Swag Holders**
DESIGNER: Amy Engman
ILLUSTRATOR: Jil Johänson
PHOTOGRAPHER: Carl Tremblay

Faux-Embroidered Curtain
DESIGNER: Livia McRee
ILLUSTRATOR: Jil Johänson
PHOTOGRAPHER: Carl Tremblay

Chandelier Dressing
DESIGNER: Dawn Anderson
ILLUSTRATOR: Jil Johänson
PHOTOGRAPHER: Carl Tremblay

Fabric-Covered Lampshade
DESIGNER: Genevieve Sterbenz
ILLUSTRATOR: Jil Johänson
PHOTOGRAPHER: Carl Tremblay

Custom "Printed" Director's Chair
DESIGNER: Nancy Overton
ILLUSTRATOR: Judy Love
PHOTOGRAPHER: Carl Tremblay

Plaid Silk Footstool
DESIGNER: Francoise Hardy
ILLUSTRATOR: Judy Love
PHOTOGRAPHER: Carl Tremblay

Relaxed-Fit Slipcover
DESIGNER: Candie Frankel
ILLUSTRATOR: Mary Newell DePalma
PHOTOGRAPHER: Carl Tremblay